Teaching
Structured Programming
in the
Secondary Schools

Teaching
Structured Programming
in the
Secondary Schools

by

Dr. Pat McIntyre
Allentown College
of
Saint Francis de Sales
Allentown, Pennsylvania

KRIEGER PUBLISHING COMPANY
MALABAR, FLORIDA
1991

Original Edition 1991

Printed and Published by
KRIEGER PUBLISHING COMPANY
KRIEGER DRIVE
MALABAR, FLORIDA 32950

Library of Congress Cataloging-in-Publication Data

McIntyre, Pat.
  Teaching Structured Programming in the Secondary Schools /
    Pat McIntyre. — Original ed.
    p. cm.
  Includes bibliographies.
  ISBN 0-89464-360-6 (alk. paper)
  1. Electronic data processing—Study and teaching. I. Title.
QA76.27.M39 1991   88-37600
004'.07'1273—dc19   CIP

10 9 8 7 6 5 4 3 2

CONTENTS

PREFACE

Reading the popular press of the educational community concerning the application of computer technology across the curriculum, one would get the impression that the teaching of the use of computer applications software is the only activity going on in the schools. The fact is that the teaching of programming is still the most significant use of the computer in the K-12 setting. What makes this even more startling is the consensus among those who have applied their analytical and research skills to the task of validating what is the state-of-the-art of teaching programming. Most of the research in this area indicates that programming is poorly taught, and offers little proof that programming accomplishes its most heralded objective of making students better problem solvers.

If I had shared these opinions before reviewing the literature on teaching programming, this book would probably never have been written. Holding these opinions does not necessarilly mean that one forsakes the teaching of programming. Programming will continue to be taught, and there is a body of knowledge that can assist teachers in being more effective in how and what they teach. There is also that lingering, intuitive perception that students do learn from their experiences with programming despite the lack of empirical confirmation. I am a better programming teacher from what I have learned in preparing this book, and I hope what I have found to share will move the study of programming forward in some modest way.

This book is for those interested in the teaching of computer science at the junior high school and high school level. It brings together what is known about novice's understandings of programming, and presents some of the ideas emerging about the teaching of computer science.

The book addresses issues on (1) goals, objectives and strategies for teaching computer science, (2) concepts of structured programming that might be taught in introductory courses, and (3) merits of different programming languages for beginners. It also includes a review of those elements of instruction that might help the preservice and inservice teacher of computer science.

In part, the text is a response to the confusion found among pre-college teachers who are called upon to teach computer science, many of whom, through no fault of their own, have limited or fragmented knowledge of the field. The book might be particularly helpful to the junior high teacher whose preparation for teaching programming might have been limited to a single course or workshop who would like to get a broader prospective of the field.

The chapters can be considered independent modules. Some will appeal more to some readers than others. The chapter on teaching program, for example, might be profitable reading for computer science instructors at any level, because the research cited on novice learners is not common knowledge. The chapter on structured programming draws together information that is not readily available to those outside the field of software engineering. Taken as a whole, the book provides enough information for an upper division or graduate level course in the teaching of computer science, although it would lack the level of true graduate preparation if the student is not provided the opportunity to review the original research reports upon which the text is based.

This book does not try to define computer science for the pre-college environment, but it does present a pragmatic view of what is happening or could happen in the school setting. This approach to pre-college computer science may tend to yield a fuzzy image of computer science as an academic discipline when compared to the more vigorous distinctions being drawn at the college and graduate levels; that is the nature of the computer science curriculum in the pre-college setting.

Some readers may take exception to some views expressed about the role of particular languages and the research on problem solving. I had hoped that through the preparation of this text, some systematic or consistent approach to the teaching of problem solving through programming would emerge. Unfortunately, the available information is fragmented and frequently not well supported by research. The teaching of problem-solving skills *may* be accomplished through the teaching of computer science, but a firm research base is lacking, and a detailed plan for how a research base might be established is yet to be articulated. While waiting for a clearer definition of problem solving, and definitive support for the teaching of programming as a means of teaching problem solving, the computer science teacher should seek out what is known. This book should help in this quest whether you are a beginning teacher writing your first lesson plan, or a fifteen-year veteran trying to increase your effectiveness.

I cannot conclude without thanking my friends and colleagues who have encouraged me in the writing of the book and who have supplied feedback on those materials that I have shared with them. Special thanks to Dr. Les Blackwell of Western Washington University, Dr. Bill Yates of the University of Kansas at Emporia, Mr. Karl Jahns of the North Kitsap School District, and Mr. John Meinke of Allentown College of Saint Francis de Sales.

CHAPTER 1
COMPUTER SCIENCE EDUCATION IN THE HIGH SCHOOL

The emergence of a new discipline is unusual in academia; the inclusion of a new subject area in the high school curriculum is unprecedented in recent memory. The basic high school curriculum has remained essentially the same since 1918. Traditional high school subjects have weathered the course of time. Even in those segments of the curriculum which are tied directly to the workplace, the changes have been minimal by almost any standard.

True, the content of science classes and mathematics classes may change to include the introduction of new topics or foci; but the general strategies, paradigms, and methodologies of the academic disciplines remain almost immutable. The immediate perceptions and needs of society may call for new and modern topics, but the high school curriculum remains true to the tenets of the established disciplines. The static nature of the high school curriculum is somewhat surprising in that the responsibility for the curriculum often rests with the numerous local school boards that represent our communities; however, the real power that controls the curriculum is often the colleges with their entrance requirements and the textbook companies with vested commercial interest. Overall, the structure of the high school curriculum has not changed much since the U.S. Bureau of Education Commission on the Reorganization of Secondary Education report in 1918.

This seemingly monolithic establishment is facing, in the early 1990s, the prospect of real change. Computer science is emerging as a new and discrete discipline. To understand and appreciate computer science as a course of study for the high school curriculum, one needs to know something about the background and forces that have placed this new discipline before our schools.

The study and use of computers is no longer considered a

1

mere extension of mathematics. Computer science is developing as a separate field of study with its own evolving purviews and protocols. As a discipline, its evolution has been both rapid and far-ranging. Computer science, which started out as a technological response to complex and lengthy numerical problems, has changed into an area of study which addresses such widely diverse issues as artificial intelligence, worldwide communications, and intellectual partnership. Considering that the first computers became commercially available in the mid-fifties and the microcomputer did not become widely available until the late seventies, the rate of change is dramatic even to the most naive observer.

The historical development of computer science as a discipline is not of primary concern to the computer science teacher, but it is appropriate and prudent to place the advent of the discipline as a high school subject into a historical perspective. In periods of rapid change, events and opinions need to be viewed in context, otherwise their importance or impact will not be fully understood. For example, in 1983, when there were approximately half a million computers available in our schools, less than 10% of the high schools had 15 or more computers. Recommendations for maximum utilization of computers in schools were very different then later. In 1985, there were over a million computers available and many high schools (over 56%) had more than 15 computers (Becker 1986a). The time is coming when there will be sufficient hardware in place to impact the entire K-12 curriculum.

As educators, we must acknowledge the uniqueness of the computer as a new element in our lives and those of our students. This uniqueness, and its impact, has best been explored and reported by the sociologist Sherry Turkle (1984) in her book The Second Self: Computers and the Human Spirit. She viewed the impact of the computer in a variety of computer environments, and has challenged us by her observations and conclusions:

> Most considerations of the computer describe it as rational, uniform, constrained by logic. I look at the computer in a different light, not in terms of its nature as an "analytical engine," but in terms of its "second nature" as an evocative object, an object that fascinates, disturbs equanimity, and precipitates thought. (p. 13)

Some wonder if the schools are prepared to accept an "evocative object," and they speculate on how it will survive in the school environment (Taylor and Johnson 1986). Does the school have a place for a machine that causes students to think about thinking, as suggested by Papert (1980, 19)? Can the school accept responsibility for the thoughts the computer engenders concerning the intellectual enterprise? With computers, it seems that schools are embarking on a new journey with old maps.

The control of access to computers is an issue of significance to our society. To a great extent, those who know how to use the computer will exert control. Although most would argue for computer literacy as an essential component of the education of the twenty-first century person, it is difficult to grasp the nature of the computer without an understanding of programming. And that is what this text is all about, an understanding of programming in its widest connotation and how it might best be taught in the secondary school setting.

Before we focus on the specifics, let us begin with an overview. The development of computer science education in the high school will be viewed from three perspectives; (1) hardware availability; (2) curriculum development; and (3) official recognition.

HARDWARE AVAILABILITY

According to Bukoski and Korotkin (1976, 18), those high schools involved in using computers during the early seventies typically had, at best, a single computer to work with, and it more often than not was shared with the administration. The lack of hardware throughout the seventies limited the growth of computer science in the high school curriculum. This is no longer the case.

Becker (1986a, 1) has determined that the number of computers available in the schools is now well over one million. The number of computers in the schools quadrupled in the two years from spring 1983 to spring 1985. The proportion of secondary schools with 15 or more computers has risen to over 56%. The typical computer-using high school has 21 computers.

Projections by Williams (1985, 88) are shown in Figure 1.1; they indicate that by 1990, the number of computers available in the schools will again quadruple to almost five million. What this says to the computer science teacher is that he no longer needs to be overly concerned about the accessibility of computers in the schools. Today there are sufficient computers in almost any high school to teach computer science. If there is a problem, it is not

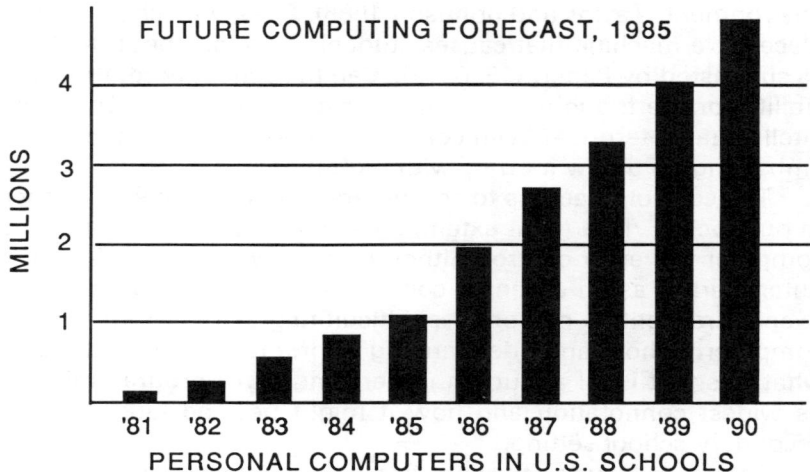

Figure 1.1. Estimate of Number of Computers in Schools (Williams, 1985)

that schools lack computers, but rather in the allocation of resources. Computer science teachers need to be prepared to argue against other legitimate reasons for using computers from CAI throughout the curriculum to the training needs of the business and vocational education departments. According to a poll in Electronic Learning (October 1987, 41) the trend in allocation of computers is to have three different laboratories in a high school: one for business, one for writing, and one for programming. The typical high school still does not have the resources to meet all these needs.

CURRICULUM DEVELOPMENT

The development of the computer science curriculum at the high school level is not as easy to trace as the availability of computers. At the beginning, the major use of computers in the high school was to teach programming. Typically, short units on programming were developed for advanced mathematics classes. When the National Council of Teachers of Mathematics prepared their report on goals for the eighties (1980), they combined computers and calculators as equivalent components of the new technology, but at that time the availability of computers was still more of a hope than a reality.

To no small degree, the curriculum has been tied to the development of the hardware and the capabilities of the machines. The availability of hardware has been the prime mover for the rapid changes in the application of the computer to classroom instruction.

For our purposes, the adaptation of the computer to the classroom will be reviewed as taking place in stages; each stage characterized by the changes in the capabilities and characteristics of the hardware.

Phase I: The Mainframes

Early applications of computers in education were limited by the fact that the computers only had the capacity to produce line-text generated at a printer using ASCII characters. If a monitor was used, the screen presentations were limited to graphics generated using the standard fonts and characters of the teletype machine. There were some notable exceptions. The PLATO system made use of a high resolution screen, and IBM developed the IBM 1500 system for instructional purposes. The latter system integrated slides and sound into the workstation. Neither of these systems were widely used in the K-12 school setting. In the main, the computer was viewed as a supercalculator with limited formatting and printing capabilities.

By 1970, according to Bukoski and Korotkin (1976), over 60% of the computer usage in the high schools was in mathematics or computer science courses, and the focus was on numeric problems. The dominant programming language was BASIC. Even when the computer was used in areas other than mathematics and computer science, it is highly likely that the computer was being used to do computation as part of simulations or problem solving exercises. During Phase I, graphics were reserved for specialized machines, and text manipulation was limited to production of forms and tables for the presentation of numeric data.

Phase II: The Microcomputer

The advent of the microcomputer caused the situation to be reassessed. The potential for computers in the schools was limited by the need for hardware that would be both powerful and inexpensive. The microcomputer met these requirements in a way that could not have been imagined, even by those who developed the original machines. Not only was a machine developed that had the power to do the necessary number-crunching, but the developers had the foresight to include powerful graphic capabilities as well. In the long run, it will probably be the graphics capabilities of the microcomputer that will lead to the success of computers as a medium of instruction.

There is increasing interest in image learning: learning that relies more on the visual image than the text. As stated by Davis (1988):

> Traditionally, illustrations have been subsidiary to text in the higher learning. Visual information is being set free from its dependence on text and the consequences for education are immense, if we can learn to exploit its possibilities. (p. 352)

The first available microcomputers were the Commodore PET and the Radio Shack TRS-80 Model I; slightly later the Apple II. As was typical in those days, software was not available until much later; software always follows hardware. The producers provided the hardware, and in some cases demonstration programs, but the development of software was left to the entrepreneurs. As might be expected, the earliest software was modeled or translated from the mainframe programs. These programs did not take advantage of the graphics capabilities of the new machines, and often in the translation, their number-crunching capabilities were sacrificed in order to meet the limited memories of the microcomputer systems. It is no wonder that many of these programs were not effective on the microcomputers. But the teacher who no longer had to deliver decks of cards to the college computer center, and then return a day or so later to get the results—results that were sensitive to every misplaced comma and every card out of sequence—was delighted with the new machines.

The first computers in the classroom used cassettes for program storage, and text screens for visual output. At this point there was little that could be done with the machines but use them for teaching programming. This is not to say that this was not an exciting adventure, but the limitations were real. The curriculum was tied to the available hardware and the software that was available for that hardware. Curriculum was planned around software rather than having software developed for the curriculum.

Programming was the focus of Phase II. The microcomputer

provided independent work stations and a highly interactive mode. Clever things were done to provide graphics images using text, and CAI was developed; but the machines were still primitive.

The situation improved when the Apple computer was introduced in late 1977. The Apple computer was different from the other early commercial computers in that it had colored graphics and sound. The inventors did not have the school market in mind with these features, but in retrospect, the power of its graphics and sound may have been the reason that the Apple II computer became the computer of choice for schools.

Not only did the Apple computer provide a greater variety of outputs—text, graphics, sound—but it provided an open system which was attractive to those who wanted to modify and adapt the computer to their own needs. The Apple computer came with detailed information about the circuits and operating system which encouraged the owners to experiment with the machine at all levels. It was not a forbidden black box.

The ability to modify and adapt the Apple computer opened up its potential to the teachers and students in high schools throughout the country, and educational software began to be produced for the Apple computer in great quantity. With the production of software, software which took advantage of the graphics capabilities of the microcomputer, the shift away from programming to CAI began. The shift was also fostered by the development of the disk drive and the reduction in cost of memory.

Phase III: Memory & Graphics

The shift to microcomputers as a means of providing instruction may have seemed slow to those most active in the field at the time, but the change was really quite fast. In a few years, from 1980 to 1985, the computer took on the role as a medium of instruction, rather than an instrument to teach students about computers. Despite the lingering clamor about the quality of the CAI materials available, the priorities for computer use shifted away from "about computers" to learning "with computers".

The microcomputer provided some unique qualities as an instructional device which otherwise are not available.

First, the microcomputer provided instruction in an environment which could be highly interactive without being labor-intensive. The computer could respond to students with specific feedback based on student input and prior information about the student, an instructional task that had in the past been limited to a live teacher and/or aide.

Second, the microcomputer provided the opportunity to present graphics images that could be both motivating and instructional, and these graphic images could be used as part of the responsive, interaction feedback mentioned above.

Third, not only could the microcomputer provide graphics, but the graphics could be animated to draw attention to certain features or concepts. Under the skilled hands of a programmer, the use of animation can be an essential part of the student interaction.

One of the earliest examples of instructional use of these unique characteristics was in 1982 when Spinnaker Software made a program called "The Story Machine" available. In this program, the student writes a story using a limited vocabulary and proper syntax. As the story is written, the characters appear on the screen and act out the story. The program requires the student to incorporate proper noun-verb agreement, sentence structure, syntax, and spelling; and the student can learn the names for appropriate parts of speech. The effect is highly motivating, and the results are excellent. Unfortunately, "The Story Machine" was not typical of commercial programs in the early eighties.

The initial enthusiasm for microcomputers as an instructional device might be traced to its novelty; novelty for the teacher and novelty for the students. In the long run this is being offset by the lack of quality software and the lack of teachers trained to use the new technology. Despite the lack of demonstrated effectiveness of software on the microcomputers as an instructional device, microcomputers have been added to the schools in numbers far in excess of almost any predictions; possibly faster than the schools could adsorb them in meaningful ways. In any case the shift in focus was very quickly away from programming to CAI and to more general strategies of problem solving. With the possible exception of LOGO, the importance of programming as a subject was overshadowed by the growth in CAI. By the mid-eighties, the microcomputer was looked upon as the device for integration of computers across the curriculum. Nevertheless, at the high school level, the prime use has remained the teaching of programming.

Phase IV: The Academic Workstation

Another shift occurred when teachers started to employ the computer to assist them in the management and development of

Grade Levels	Drill & Practice	Problem Solving	Programming	Word Processing	Other
Elem	49%	9%	19%	6%	8%
Middle/ Jr. High	39%	11%	31%	16%	3%
High School	25%	12%	40%	20%	6%
U.S. Total	32%	14%	33%	15%	6%

Figure 1.2. Mean Percent of Instructional Computer Time, Spring 1985 (Becker 1986a)

instruction. The same applications software which proved the value of the microcomputer for the business workplace began to impact the teaching profession. The microcomputer became a valuable tool for the teacher in preparing classes, keeping records, and reducing the workload.

The value of the computer for students quickly emerged, and computer education emerged into Phase IV: word processing, databases and spreadsheets. This stage is characterized not so much as a move towards training for business and vocations, but rather is a move towards the utilization of the computer as a creative tool for expression and communication. According to Becker (1986a) by the spring of 1985, 15% of the instructional use of computers in schools was word processing. (See Figure 1.2)

The rapid changes in the ways that computers are being used in the schools may be settling down, but not necessarily. The microcomputer continues to grow in complexity and power. What started out as a super adding machine has evolved into a text processor that puts the potential for publication into the hands of anyone with the desire. It has evolved from a text oriented machine to a graphics medium and soon into a true pictorial mode. If the short ten-year history of microcomputers has taught us anything, it is not to underestimate what this new source of power can lead to when placed in the hands of creative people.

At the high school level, the utilization of computers has begun to fall into three distinct categories: (1) computer assisted instruction, (2) applications software, and (3) programming. The latter two categories belonged in the purview of the computer science teacher, although some might argue that applications software was the domain of the business department. According to the Becker (1986a) survey in the Spring of 1985, computer assisted instruction (Drill and Practice & Problem Solving) amounted to 26% of the computer instructional time at the high school level, applications software (Word Processing) 20%, and programming 49% (See Figure 1.2). So despite significant shifts in focus in the schools in general, the teaching of programming remains the primary mode of instructional computing at the high school level. Overall, programming remains the major instructional use at all levels—33% of the time.

What this says to the computer science teacher is that although the more innovative and instructional uses of computers have received most of the publicity over the past six or seven years, the major use of computers in the high school still is in programming classes.

There is a real need to provide quality instruction in programming. This is not to say that this will always be the case. The technology continues to advance. The next generation of microcomputers will have significantly greater capabilities for the presentation of images, and the shift will be away from graphics images to what will appear to be pictorial presentations. Pictorial presentations will be created in real time, and the user friendly environment will require no special computing skills or knowledge of the computer system being used. With greater screen resolution and faster storage access, the utilization of CD-ROM will place instructional tools in the hands of teachers that will move us ahead by another quantum jump. Even if this does happen, and the schools utilize the more advanced technology for more and more instruction, the need to introduce students to the basic elements of programming will certainly remain at its present level, but more than likely the demand will increase because of the desire to have students understand the ubiquitous machine.

OFFICIAL RECOGNITION

The teaching of computer science in the high school has been going on for 25 years or more, and yet it is not a legitimate subject. This may be a harsh statement, but as noted earlier, there have been very few new disciplines introduced into the school curriculum in the past hundred years. More often then not, new topics are incorporated into existing courses without formal recognition of their unique qualities and roles. Computer science may be another example of this accommodation; the accommodation is not without its problems. According to Taylor and Poirot (1984) the problems fall into two areas of concern—accreditation and certification.

Accreditation

All courses taught in the public schools must receive formal approval. This approval may be from a local school board, but in many cases this approval must be made by a state board level or by a professional accreditation committee or agency. There does not seem to be any opposition to approving a courses in computer science at the high school level. If anything there is a concern that there are not enough courses available for students. "Computer literacy" as a goal for all students is widely held and formal approval by most local and state boards of education or other agencies responsible for public school curriculum is easily gained.

The problem with accreditation is with the classification and "ownership" of courses in computer science. There is no mechanism for the establishment of new disciplines as valid, independent fields within the public school curriculum. Computer science, although a recognized subject area, is often assigned to other areas of the curriculum. In many cases, computer science has been placed under the purview of the mathematics department and the courses are viewed as mathematics courses, but this approach is not without its opponents. In recent years, the business departments of many high schools have laid claim to instruction about the microcomputer as being within their range of responsibilities. The battle is just beginning, but it will be an administrator's problem of the first magnitude before it is resolved.

The responsibility for the courses is not without significant curriculum implications. When a course is identified as a mathematics course, the problem of deciding whether or not it replaces a more traditional mathematics courses surfaces as well as do issues of what mathematics courses will be prerequisites. In the latter case, it is well known that some mathematics departments require a year of algebra before studying programming. Such requirements limit the availability of the courses to a restricted audience. These are issues that can be resolved, but the resolution may not be in the best interest of the prime subject area or of the students.

Placing the computer science courses in the business department results in similar problems. The course naturally takes on a more occupational focus, and can become part of a series of clerically oriented courses. For example, in one school district the computer programming class has as a prerequisite a year of typing. This same district has reported a decline in the interest in programming courses.

The placement of computer courses in the academic program raises professional as well as planning issues.

Certification

The move towards recognizing the special preparation required to teach computer science has been slow, but the trend is certainly clear. Each year more and more states are approving courses of study and requirements for certification of computer science teachers. The Association for Computing Machinery (ACM) (Task Force on Teacher Certification in Computer Science 1985) has established guidelines for certification, and the National Association of State Directors of Teacher Education and Certification (NASDTEC) (1981) has proposes a list of competencies for computer science teachers. The political process is slow, but it is reasonable to assume that before the mid-1990s a majority of states will have an approved certification program for computer science teachers.

Having a certificate to teach computer science does not solve the problem for a new teacher. If the related issues of accreditation and ownership are not resolved, the computer science teacher will find that he is a member of the mathematics department or the business department. Considering the size of most high schools, and the limited number of programming classes that will be taught, having a single "legal" subject to teach may place the computer science teacher at a real disadvantage on the job market. Thus, for the immediate future, high school computer science teachers will need to have proper credentials in more than one field.

The trend towards certification of computer science teachers has been acknowledged by NASDTEC. This association sets standards for those state certification offices who agree to recognize each others certifications so that teachers can move among the states without fear of losing their credentials. Through this process, which is known as reciprocity, a teacher who holds certification in one of the thirty-two states that has signed the agreement may feel free to move about without fear of losing his vested interest in the original certification program.

The NASDTEC standards emphasize problem solving, structured programming, program design, and computer systems. The standards are presented in Appendix A. It is safe to say that the level of competence suggested by the association exceeds the level of knowledge of many high school computer science teachers, but as goals, the standards present a challenge to those preparing to teach.

COMMENTARY

The history of computers in the schools goes back only a few years. Most high schools acquired their first computer for academic work in the early eighties. The majority of schools did not have a significant number of microcomputers until about 1985, and these computers serve a variety of purposes: drill and practice, problem solving, programming and word processing. Available resources and the manner in which computers are used in the schools is in a constant state of flux.

A serious question still remains. "Is the microcomputer going to live up to its potential in the schools?" Many of the innovations of the past 25 years have not reached their expected potential: programmed instruction, modular scheduling, individualized programs, and educational television to name a few. Microcomputers may suffer the same decline. At the present time activity in the allocation of hardware and the development of software is still in an upward spiral, but schools do not readily adjust to change. It almost seems that if computers are going to reach their potential in education, the schools will have to change.

Issues surrounding accreditation and certification are likely to bring political pressure on the proponents of computer science as those in the established fields seek to protect their territories. When computers are used to augment the present instructional program, professional groups are not threatened, but when a new course is proposed as a high school requirement, we are looking at a shift of as much as 5% of the total high school curriculum. The 5% of the curriculum must come from some other curriculum area. A new consensus must emerge if we are to continue in a forward direction.

RECOMMENDED READINGS

William J. Bukoski and Arthur L. Korotkin, "Computing Activities in Secondary Education." *Educational Technology*, Vol. 16, No. 1, January 1976, pp. 9–23. A detailed report and comparison of the state of computer science in the schools in 1970 and 1975.

Harriet G. Taylor and James L. Poirot, "Computer Science Teacher Certification: Current Status and Trends." *T.H.E Journal*, Vol. 12, No. 2, September 1984, pp. 103–107. Although the information on what states have certification is dated, the presentation of the various ways states have addressed the issue of certification is important reading. The discussion of the relationship between certification and accreditation is very revealing.

"New Languages for Problem Solving" in *Understanding Computers: Software.* Time-Life Books, Alexandria, Virginia, 1985, pp. 25–56.

"A Golden Age of Entrepreneurship" in *Understanding Computers: Computer Basics*. Time-Life Books, Alexandria, Virginia, 1985, pp. 93–121. Interesting anecdotes about the beginnings of the development of computer software for the microcomputer. Excellent material for supplementing lectures or providing short readings for students.

Ernest L. Boyer, "Technology: Extending the Teacher's Reach," in *High School: A Report on Secondary Education in America*. Harper and Row, New York, 1983, pp. 186–201. A review of how other technologies have been responded to by the school community, and some thought about prospects for the computer in the educational environment.

Sherry Turkle, *The Second Self: Computers and the Human Spirit*. Simon and Shuster, New York, 1984. An excellent sociological exploration of the impact of computers on various people from young children to the new philosophers.

Jack Culbertson and Luvern L. Cunningham (Eds.), *Microcomputers and Education*. Eighty-fifth Yearbook of the National Society for the Study of Education, Chicago, 1986. A scholarly and thoughtful probe and analysis of educational policies concerning the use of microcomputers in the schools.

SUGGESTED ACTIVITIES

1. Obtain a copy of the certification requirements for computer science teachers in your state and write a paper comparing it to the competencies recommended by the Association for Computing Machinery [*Proposed Curriculum for Programs Leading to Teacher Certification in Computer Science*. Communications of Association for Computing Machinery, Vol. 28, No. 3, March 1985, pp. 275–279] or the National Association of State Directors of Teacher Education and Certification (Appendix A).

2. Arrange for representatives of the mathematics and business departments of a local high school to attend one of your classes and discuss how they view their responsibilities with respect to teaching computer science and/or computer literacy.

3. Prepare a position paper which presents your views on what the minimum requirements should be for a "computer literate" high school graduate, and support your view with not less than five authoritative opinions.

4. Write a short paper on the impact of the introduction of the IBM-PC on the utilization of computers in the schools.

5. Write a short paper on the potential impact of the introduction of the NEXUS computer on instructional computing.

CHAPTER 2
TEACHING PROGRAMMING

What do we know about how novices learn programming? Do we have anything better than informal observations to use as the basis for developing an instructional program? Research on teaching programming is no better than educational research in general, and probably it is not even as good. Nevertheless, a body of information is slowly building.

Educational computing research suffers from the same problems that face other areas of instructional research, and it has the added burden of novelty, "hype", and "research expertise". Exposing students to a cognitively rich environment in which they have some control is certainly going to effect their attitudes and disposition but it is unclear how long the novelty will impact learning. According to Clark (1985) the evidence is that the effect of novelty wears off in elementary school in about a year, and in the high school in even less time. The acceptance of computers into the school is in no small way traceable to the enthusiasm engendered by books like Mindstorms (Papert 1980) and the promise of technological advantages in the workplace for students with computer skills; this enthusiasm has created expectations that have yet to be validated. The classroom teacher as a consumer of research results needs to be wary of those who have a vested interest in reporting or publishing significant findings.

This is not to say that the literature is lacking in information and insight into the teaching of programming, but the caveat needs to be observed, lest the effectiveness of programming in education be elevated to a degree that it has not earned. Most objective critics would say this has already occurred with the teaching of LOGO.

There are a few things that can be said with some confidence about the teaching of programming to new programmers, and the researchers have occasionally offered some special insight into the process or the environment for teaching programming. In this chapter, an attempt will be made to take the research findings about teaching programming and show how they might help a teacher be more effective.

For readers who might not be familiar with the problems of educational research, we will first consider why some of the research is so poor; this will alert the unwary to claims that may not be proven in practice. Many researchers in the field of computers in education seem to be new to the task of research. They seem to have great difficulty in developing a controlled experiment, and often ignore accepted process and procedures.

Let us take as an example the research reported by Webb (1985, 190):

> The findings of no difference between the group and individual learning settings on any programming outcome showed that students are not disadvantaged when they work in groups to learn computer programming.

This statement certainly has curriculum implications, and may appeal to those with budget constraints on the hardware needs of their students. The author (Webb 1985) suggests:

> The use of group work would also make it possible to give a larger number of students exposure to computers and for a longer period. (p. 190)

As much as we might like to be able to state this conclusion, an examination of the report shows the following problems:

1. The students in the study were not typical; they were paid volunteers who were recruited using flyers distributed in ten elementary schools, junior high schools and through advertisement in local newspapers.
2. The entire instructional program took place in a single three-hour session on one afternoon. The topics included "the operating system, input and output commands, logical relations, branching, looping, data types, arithmetic operators, and relationships."
3. The instructional material was developed by the author for the study, and no evidence was provided on its curriculum validity.
4. The instructional mode was atypical. The materials were designed to be self-sufficient and self-pacing.
5. The outcomes were measured by a test for which no content validity was offered. The test had twenty-six items designed

to measure four programming outcomes; each outcome was scored independently. Reliability was presented for the overall test, but subtests were used in the statistical analysis.

6. The "group setting" consisted of pairs of students who were instructed to work with each other, ask each other for help, and consult with the instructor only if neither student could proceed. There was no evidence reported on whether they did consult, and no evidence was provided to support the assumption that they did indeed work on the computer together. It is possible that there was no group treatment.

It is not necessary to go into the statistical analysis that was done to pursue the possibility of detecting spurious relationships. If this were an atypical research report, it would not be of concern, but in fact, much reported in the literature is of similar value. The research was done at a research institute, and it was published in a recognized journal. Clark (1985, 146), although he was more concerned with computer assisted instruction (CAI), may be right in his assertion that there is bias among journal editors when it comes to publishing articles on the effects of computers on learning. Published research may not have been done as rigorously as acceptance by a journal would imply.

In reviewing the research, it became apparent that a number of researchers had a continuing interest in the teaching of programming. Much of what follows can be traced to this core group of researchers. In most cases, the conclusions are based on a continuing series of experiments, and/or a particular insight that might be taken as especially valuable because it stems from a body of work. For example, Linn (1985) reported on a fairly extensive project in which students from six junior high schools were tested on their understanding of certain features of BASIC. The results were not very encouraging, based on a model of cognitive accomplishments: most students were found to be at the lowest level, and no evidence indicated that students were learning problem-solving skills. A question arose about the quality of the instruction in the schools, with the result that two schools with exemplary programs were appended to the study. In the analysis and discussion of the results, it was reported that the teachers in the two exemplary programs had extensive preparation in teaching programming, while the teachers in the typical schools may have had no more than a single workshop on the topic. The design of the study, already adjusted by the addition of two schools, could not take into account the difference in training, nor the differences in other potentially confounding variables. The report, however, sends a message that needs to be heard—in looking at research on student achievement in programming, attention should be paid to the professional preparation of teachers, as it may be a very significant confounding variable if not controlled.

Over time, it may be possible to identify the most significant variables and true experimental studies may be done. Meanwhile, the collection of data on novice programmers and the development of instructional resources and strategies borrowed from other areas of the curriculum should enable us to approach the teaching of programming in a reasonably professional manner.

Meanwhile, a questioning attitude is suggested for research findings based on (1) small selective samples; (2) those on subjects with less than fifty hours of instruction; and (3) evaluation instruments lacking established validity or reliability.

PROGRAMMING CONCEPTS

What is the present status of instruction in programming? Many teachers seem to see teaching programming as a process of introducing the students to a set of commands showing the proper syntax for the commands, and then, through examples or assignments, having the students use the commands to write programs or program segments. Over a period of time, the commands get more powerful, the assignments more complex, and the student responses more productive and creative. However, the issue of teaching more general problem-solving skills or laying a foundation for transfer of learning to other programming languages is not addressed.

Students should learn a specific language to use as a conceptual model of programming. The actual language taught should be within the framework of an overview of what programming is all about. It may be that a student will never learn another language, but he should be provided with the basic principles of programming. Ideally it would not be necessary to learn a special language in order to communicate with a computer, but for the foreseeable future it will remain a necessity. As long as it is necessary, our job is to provide the best possible instruction.

In the pursuit of that goal, we will be looking at a hierarchical model which is built around (1) syntax, (2) sequence, and (3) context. The pieces of the model, and the rationale for its use in instructing beginning programmers will be presented before some of the detailed functional aspects of teaching programming are described.

This chapter assumes that the reader is familiar with at least one higher-level language. The concepts are presented as they might be classified in a taxonomy, not as they would be introduced in an introductory programming course. The information is organized to assist in developing a framework or conceptual map of programming not tied to specific languages or syntax. These are the general concepts that must be instilled in students if our goal is for learning to be transferable to other languages and/or problem-solving situations.

Syntax

The lowest level of programming is the writing and interpreting of individual lines of code. Working at this level, an instructor usually introduces a command and has his student become actively involved in using the command either through demonstrations or practice. At some point, the limitations or conditions required of the command are presented. For example, the PRINT command might be introduced and the syntax for printing out strings would be shown. At first no limitations would be mentioned, but depending on the level and experience of the student, limitations such as the maximum string length or the use of hidden characters would be presented.

Some teachers might choose to have the students experiment with the command to determine the limitations rather than having them learn in a more passive manner; some teachers make use of an immediate mode to facilitate this learning. But whatever way it is done, the student, at some point, needs to have his knowledge confirmed or be given the precise syntax of the command.

The student should be aware that the syntax of the language must be precise—often with little flexibility, and frequently with well-defined limits. The use of English words as commands should make syntax easy to learn, but as pointed out by duBoulay (1986,

62) this is not always the case for novices, who might use any of several acceptable meanings for common terms. For example, the term THEN could be interpreted to mean "after"; the Boolean operator AND might be interpreted as joining together a sequence of actions. REPEAT suggests to a novice that something in existence is to be repeated.

It helps at this level to have the computer language as close to natural language as possible, but care must be taken to avoid language that can be misinterpreted. In an interesting study of young children's use of mental models to explain LOGO routines, Kurland and Pea (1985, 242) found that the use of STOP and END as commands in LOGO mislead students to think that these commands stopped or ended the program rather than passing the control back to some other segment of the program. This problem will increase as languages get to be more "natural."

An instructor has little control over the choice of reserved words or commands in the language, but he ought to appreciate the cognitive problems that naive students have when a common term is used in a very restricted way. Some of these difficulties can be avoided by having a good understanding of such semantic problems in advance.

Bonar and Soloway (1985, 1) have observed that in writing programs, novices fill in gaps in their programming knowledge by inappropriate use of typical English syntax and grammar, what they chose to call "informal natural language procedures." When confronted with constructs they do not understand, or with a programming impasse, students tend to resort to natural language interpretations and assign the machine the reasoning power of an average human.

If a problem exists with programming as taught in our schools, it is that too much time and effort is spent on the particulars of syntax. Although the trend is towards more formal instruction for computer science teachers, most are self-taught. The problem stems from the fact that their knowledge is often limited to the syntax they learned from the instructional manuals that accompany the computers.

It is interesting that the authors of BASIC, Kemeny and Kurtz (1985, 9) designed BASIC so as to require "no understanding of the hardware", and it is often taught that way, but Mayer (1979) has demonstrated that without an understanding of what goes on inside the computer students are often at a loss to understand the syntax of a language.

Sequence

The second level in the conceptualization of a program concerns the sequencing of program lines. No matter what language is being taught, the instructor needs to establish from early on that the computer follows a controlled sequence of commands organized within the program. The sequence is prepared by the programmer using a limited number of control functions. Sequence is an overriding concept.

The importance of sequence presents a basic cognitive program for the novice; a problem that might not be all that apparent. For example, given the following problem:

$$A = B$$
$$B = 4$$

What would be the value of A? The obvious answer is A = 4, and if the question had been asked in an algebra class, it would be correct. But if the same lines appeared in a program, that is

```
10   A = B
20   B = 4
30   PRINT A
```

The result would not be 4; it would be 0. The difference in the two cases is that, in the first, the equations are considered simultaneously; in the second case, the equations are treated sequentially.

Pea (1986, 25) calls this type of error the "parallelism bug." The programmer assumes that certain lines are active after the control of the program has gone on to other lines. He sites the case where an IF statement appears early in a sequence, and then later the condition of the IF is met. Eight out of ten students in a study thought that the IF statement was still active and was "waiting for" the condition to be met. Some students have the idea that all programming lines, once processed, remain active throughout the program.

A similar phenomenon was observed by Soloway et al. (1981, 206), who reported on the tendency of novice Pascal programmers to assume that during the execution of a WHILE loop, the condition was monitored after each command was executed. The students interpreted WHILE as being consistent with natural usage in English. Students attribute more to the computer than it is capable of doing. They assume the computer is capable of the natural language discourse and simultaneous considerations, rather than being limited to a very strict sequencing of events controlled by a formal syntax. (It should be noted that with the advent of certain "natural languages" such as Prolog, the role of sequence may be handled by rules inferred by a compiler or interpreter; the simple concept of sequence will be confounded by parallel processing.)

The sequence of data input is a problem that is often overlooked by computer science teachers. Algebra teachers have been teaching students that problems were solved on the assumption that all the conditions held for the whole problem—variables didn't necessarily vary. The computer science teacher teaches a different concept; each command is executed in sequence, and any changes in conditions need to be explicitly made. A student will have trouble knowing when he needs to think of operations as being simultaneous and when to consider them as sequential.

On the other hand, the necessity for sequence in programming can be so overemphasized that sometimes students are not sensitive to either conditional or unconditional branching.

In most approaches to structured programming, the format of the listing has built-in visual clues to make it easier for the student to see where the changes in sequence or control occur. As will be discussed later, the use of unconditional branching, that is, the use of the GOTO command, is one of the major complaints about the most common forms of BASIC. Teachers should encourage their students to limit, if not eliminate, the use of the GOTO command by better organization of the modules within their programs. This will increase clarity, since the sequence of steps becomes more evident.

Some instructors suggest that in organizing a program, the coding should begin with the various subroutines followed by the main program. This is done to make the execution of the program more efficient, because when a subroutine call is used within a program, the listing is searched from the beginning to locate the appropriate line number of the subroutine. Having the subroutines at the top of the listing means the program runs more efficiently.

This practice requires that the program begin with an unconditional command to jump to the main program, and this results in a program listing which does not conform to the logical flow of the program. For beginning programmers, these are unnecessary distractions which can cause confusion. As pointed out by Joni and Soloway (1986) efficiency may be an important consideration for expert programmers, but it only interferes with the learning of programming by the novice.

An instructor must repeatedly go back to the idea that <u>a computer executes a program according to the sequence of commands written in the program</u>, and that this sequence can be varied through the use of specific control commands and structures. In some cases, the commands are passive, in that when they occur, the computer shifts to a predetermined location; for example, the RETURN command at the end of a subroutine in BASIC. In other cases, the sequence of program lines is controlled by conditions set within the program that are examined prior to execution; for example, the IF/THEN GOTO command.

Kurland and Pea (1985, 242) detected the tendency of some children to assume from looking at one line of code what the following lines will do without actually reading them. This does not mean that the students did not understand that the computer would follow the lines in the order given, provided there wasn't a branch command, but rather that there is a tendency to overgeneralize from one line of code to a sequence of familiar code without actually exploring the sequence of commands as written. The sequencing of code leads us to the next level of the hierarchy, the programming context of a line of code.

Context

Since programming must be done line by line and the sequencing of commands is a prominent consideration, the beginning programmer often seems to think that all he or she needs to do is to learn the individual commands and the rest of programming will fall into place. In order to produce programs of more than a few lines of code, the programmer must understand the importance of the context of a line in a program. Students most become "context-sensitive" if they are going to be able to write meaningful code.

The argument for "context-sensitivity" is supported by the research by Kurland and Pea (1985) in which they asked young children to explain what a particular procedure involving recursion would do. They made the following observation that can be generalized to naive programmers in a variety of situations:

They (children) attempt to understand each line of programming code individually, ignoring the context provided by previous lines. They stated the definition of each command, rather than treating program lines as parts of a functional structure in which the purpose of particular lines is context-sensitive and sequence-dependent (p. 236).

The focus on syntax and sequence can lead a student to think that each line of code is independent, when in fact each line must be viewed as part of a whole, either the entire program or a particular program segment. It is not unusual for a student to understand each of the commands in a program segment, and yet have no idea of its total or composite function.

One of the advantages of a structured programming approach is that the structured program provides visual clues to the context of a particular line of code. It may be that teaching a structured approach is more efficient because it focuses on context.

It is worth noting that Pascal was originally written as an instructional language, not as a "programmer's" or systems language. Wirth's motivation was to develop a language that could be used to instill good programming style and form. The formalized style and form of Pascal may be the reason that it has turned out to be an efficient language to learn. Clearly, modular programming and the use of local and global variables are concepts that need clarification and understanding, but once understood, these concepts can help the student appreciate the importance of context in analyzing a programming segment. One of the advantages of Pascal is that the concepts of local and global variables are explicitly taught, and in the process the concept of context-sensitivity is learned, even if not made explicit by the teacher. A good teacher will constantly draw the students' attention to the context of lines of code that are being analyzed.

Success at programming may be traced to a novice's ability to balance the concepts of "context-sensitivity" and "sequence-dependency." A teacher needs to be aware of these concepts, and assist the student in differentiating between them in the analysis of a program. When a student has a problem with a program segment, it is helpful for the teacher to determine whether the problem is due to a lack of understanding of the sequence of events, or the context of the program. The correction of the syntax should be done within the context of these considerations.

Part of the teaching of programming as problem solving requires the teaching of debugging. One debugging strategy is to ask the question: "is the problem with syntax, sequence, or context?" This seems almost too simple, but novices often lack a firm knowledge of syntax and tend to focus on it as the primary source of error when a program does not perform as expected. They need to be taught to consider the other two options.

Being sensitive to context and sequence of a line are not the only problems for novices. Pea (1986) points out that students often look at a segment of code, and infer some goal or foresightedness to it. They adopt what is called an "intentional stance", which assumes the computer knows what it is doing even if the lines of code are not exactly right. This occurs because the student looks ahead at a sequence of commands and, recognizing a familiar pattern, assumes what the computer will do. In fact, even though the syntax may be similar, the actual program may be for something very different.

A similar phenomenon occurs when novices are writing programs. Students assume that the computer knows what they intend to have it do, and that the commands are sufficient to accomplish this end. Pea (1986, 30) calls these "egocentrism bugs" which lead to the writing of programs that are not "fleshed out." One might think that such errors are due to mere omissions on the part of the student, but it is argued that this is not the case. Students have difficulty determining the amount of help that a computer can provide; they have trouble because of the tendency to use a human conversational metaphor in programming.

PROGRAMMING SYNTAX

The teaching of programming is often reduced to the teaching of the syntax of the language, and the student is expected to learn the general ideas and concepts on his own. If, as is commonly suggested, an important goal of teaching computer programming is to develop problem-solving skills, then the courses need to be more than just an introduction to the syntax of a language. In fact, an introductory course might be language independent, except that this might lead to unnecessary confusion when students are required to write code.

In order for students to master problem-solving skills, the skills must be taught explicitly by the instructor. Students need to be taught general concepts, as well as specific information. In the presentation that follows, specific commands will be organized under broader concepts. In a sense, the commands will be structured into a taxonomy of commands and functions that might be addressed in an introductory computer course.

This should not be interpreted as a suggestion that the teaching of a language must follow the sequence presented. The logic of presentation in a class is typically dependent on the programming tasks used to introduce a student to the language; this can be very different from the logic of the language. A teacher has many opportunities to summarize and articulate how the various commands are subsumed under more general concepts. If the more general concepts are conveyed to the students, it will make the transfer of learning between languages much easier.

Variables

The single most difficult concept for many naive programmers is that of variables. The simple concept of a variable, not just keeping track of variables or how to assign values to them, is hard to grasp. Some high school courses require algebra before programming because they have found that a grade in algebra is a good indicator of success in programming. Some suggest that learning programming first is an aid to learning algebra. If this is the case, it is probably due to the introduction of the concept of variables. It may be that this can be traced to the ability of students to understand what a variable is. It is difficult for a student to learn what a variable is and how it functions while at the same time trying to learning how a computer handles variables.

The term "variable" itself is not without its semantic difficulties. In common usage, people intend the term "variable" to stand for something that changes, and often there is no control over the changes. The term, when partially understood, can mean something that can change its value in a random and unpredictable way. If most people are asked to give an example of a variable, they might respond "the weather." This is not a useful concept for programming.

In any case, a computer science teacher must be aware that some, if not most, students will have trouble with the variable concept. The beginning problem is that students have trouble distinguishing between the name of a variable and its value, the name being a constant, and the value being the thing that is changeable. Notice that it was not said that the value of a variable changes, but that it is changeable, meaning that the value is determined and not arbitrary. This is simple to say, but it is not a trivial notion.

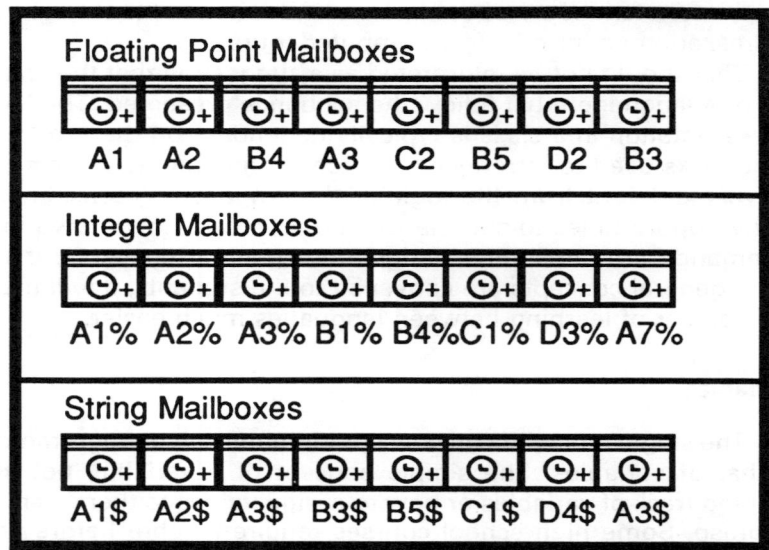

FIGURE 2.1. *The Mailbox Analogy for Variables Storage*

The standard visualization of this concept makes use of the mailbox analogy (Figure 2.1). In this analogy the name of the variable is the location of the mailbox, and the information in the mailbox is the value of the variable. This is a widely used analogy, and for someone who understands variables, it probably works well; but as Mayer (1979, 592) has pointed out, where students have trouble is in understanding the process inside the computer when a variable is assigned a value. He suggests the student should be given some idea of what is going on inside the computer when a variable is being used.

The understanding is probably hindered by the extensions of the concept which include the fact that there are a variety of types of variables, and more than one way in which a variable can be assigned a value. These ideas will be discussed separately.

Types of Variables. Not only is there a problem with variables, but, in even the simplest of systems, more than one type of variable is used. Within the computer, the various types of variables are processed in several ways; in particular, the values of different types of variables are not stored in the same manner or the same areas of the computer's memory.

With this in mind, it is suggested that the mailbox analogy

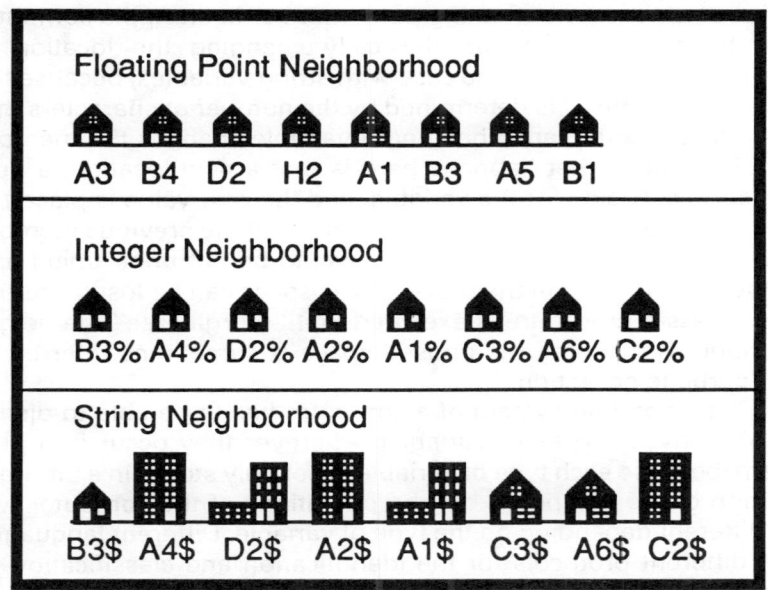

FIGURE 2.2. *The House Analogy for Variable Storage*

might be replaced by a house analogy (Figure 2.2). In this analogy, the type of variable to be stored determines the neighborhood of the house where it is stored, and the name indicates the address within the neighborhood. In a particular neighborhood there is only one type of house and only one type value can be stored in the houses. The neighborhood refers to a portion of memory allocated for a type of variable.

In the Apple II computer, for example, there would be three neighborhoods corresponding to string, integer, and floating point variables. The house types in two of these neighborhoods are fixed in size; they take up seven memory locations and are located directly below that portion of memory which contains the disk operating system (Poole 1981, 352). Because of the fixed size of the houses, seven memory locations, the magnitude of the numbers is limited to what can be stored in the units. This is not the case with string variables, because in their "neighborhood" the houses are built to accommodate the value of the string. There are usually limitations to the size of strings that can be stored in a variable; in the case of the Apple II, this would be 254 characters.

Pushing this analogy a little further, it can be noted that the value of an integer or floating point number in an Apple computer can be changed without physically changing the location in memory, but this is not the case with string variables, because the size of the "house" is determined by the number of characters that need to be stored, and changing a variable changes the memory requirements. What happens here is that a new location, a new house, is set aside for the variable, and the new value is placed in the new location. It might be pointed out that the previous memory locations allocated to the variable would be left unoccupied and without an address in the process. The space can be lost for future use unless a procedure is executed that "reorganizes" the neighborhood. Reclaiming the unused space is sometimes referred to as "garbage collection."

The operating system of a computer has to be able to distinguish between types of variables wherever they occur in a program, because each type of variable is not only stored in a different portion of the computer, but the operations of the computer will be different depending on the type of variable. Different languages use different protocols for the identification and classification of variables.

Frequently, variations in dialects of BASIC have to do with the identification of variable types. In Microsoft BASIC, the last character in the variable name is used as the type identifier, whereas in Pascal it is customary to have the variable's type declared as part of the initialization of the program. In the latter case, it then becomes possible to define new types of variables that might be more efficient. In terms of the house analogy, it is possible to define new types of neighborhoods.

Assigning Values to Variables. It is one thing to have the concept of a variable, and yet another to deal with the process of how a value is assigned to a variable. Putnam et al (1986), have pointed out that one of the most common mistakes made by programmers has to do with their inability to understand the incrementing of a counter: i.e., $C = C + 1$. The problem with this notation is that it is contrary to normal algebraic notation, and it does not imply anything about what is happening inside the computer.

It is suggested that to begin with the explicit use of the LET command, although it isn't required, helps explain incrementation to the naive user. This understanding can be further improved by making sure that the student recognizes that the symbol = does not mean equal but rather is used as a means of assigning a value to a variable, and then finally, the student needs to know that it is not the variable C that is of interest but rather the value of the variable that needs to be considered. Mayer (1979) suggests that it is a good idea to explain the process that takes place within the computer as a means of adding understanding to this expression.

A teacher should clearly establish the difference between the name of a variable and its value. The use of the LET notation can be a big help if used consistently, and read in the following way: *"Let the value of C be equal to the previous value of C plus 1."* The key to the phrasing is *"Let the value of C be equal . . . "* This is much better than saying "*C equals C plus 1*" which is simply not true for several reasons and it creates cognitive conflicts. First, C is the name of a variable, and names of variables are not added or subtracted. Second, if it were a value, the expression would not make sense algebraically.

Some instructors insist that the symbol "=" not be equated with equal under any circumstance. To emphasize the process that takes place within the computer, they insist that the symbol be interpeted as "be replaced by." *"Let the value of C be replaced by the value of C + 1."*

To beginning programmers, what is meant by the simple command $C = C + 1$ is not obvious, and it is no wonder that they have trouble interpreting its meaning. A teacher who neglects to acknowledge the possible confusion that might surround such a "simple" line of code will never understand why some students have lingering problems understanding loops and flags.

Students can have a wide range of misconceptions regarding the assignment of values to variables using the LET command. Based on interviews with fifty-six students who had taken a course in BASIC, and who had problems with certain programming statements, Putnam et al (1986) reported that (1) students reverse the assignment and let $A = B$ (B ends up with the value of A) for the statement LET $A = B$; but generally make the right assignment when given the statement LET $A = B + C$, and (2) they had trouble with LET $C = C + 1$, but had less problems with LET $C = W + 1$. They suggest that this is due to the "inappropriate imposition of reasoning and knowledge from more informal domains to the formal domain of programming." (Putnam et al. 1986, 462).

In a related experiment, Bayman and Mayer (1982, 33) reported that only 27% of the students tested had adequate explanations for the statement LET $A = B + 1$ and only 43% for LET $D = 0$. They suggest that this may be because the students were not taught explicitly the processes of a computer, and consequently failed to develop an adequate conceptual or mental model of the system.

It should be noted that in neither of the two studies mentioned above did the researchers attempt to teach the concepts that they evaluated. In the first case, the students had completed one of several courses, and in the second case, they received instruction which did <u>not</u> include the use of models. The observations merely demonstrate the kinds of misunderstandings students can have after instruction. It is hoped that with proper instruction these errors might be avoided.

A study of misunderstandings of high school students who had had a course in Pascal, reported a parallel set of errors (Sleeman et al. 1986). Although the syntax in Pascal is very different from BASIC, assignment statement and variable errors were still common.

For our purposes, the first study says it is essential the student to be made aware that the LET statement should not be viewed as an algebraic expression; the use of the = sign is an unfortunate choice of symbols and must not be interpreted literally. The second report suggests that the LET command will really not be understood unless the student is provided with explicit instruction which includes "the specific memory locations and under what conditions values stored in these locations get replaced." (Sleeman et al. 1986)

A teacher should know that although the following four lines of code are alike to the computer and experienced programmers, naive students often interpret them differently:

LET C = 0
LET C = B
LET C = C + 1
LET C = B + 1

Of course, the use of the LET command is only one of several ways that values might be assigned to variables, but the actual commands used to assign values to variables are usually very limited. In the case of BASiC only three commands--LET, INPUT, and READ--can be used to assign values to variables.

Bayman and Mayer (1982, 33) report that the most difficult statement to grasp for their subjects was INPUT A. Novice programmers had difficulty knowing where the data was to come from, and how it was stored in memory. Students also had trouble with the idea that the executive control of the computer was changed when such a command was encountered.

Putnam et al. (1986) did not investigate the students' ideas concerning the INPUT command, but reported that more of the students they interviewed had trouble with the READ statement than any other aspect of the BASIC language. Some students had the idea that the READ statement could somehow selectively take values from DATA statements. For example, if the statement was READ ODD, some thought that the computer would select an odd number from the DATA statements.

This same error was observed among Pascal students. Sleeman et al. (1986, 9) referred to the difficulty as the "semantic constrained read" error. They suggested that students read into the name of a variable certain operational qualities, when in fact they are merely labels, labels which cannot be interpreted by the computer to be anything else but a memory location. Another read error occurred in Pascal when students confused the order in which variables were declared with the order in which they were read.

Another misconception they observed was that some students thought all the values in a DATA statement were read into a single variable, and that the variable would then contain multiple values. This was the most significant misconception involving variables. A student with this fundamental misconception has little hope of success in a programming course. In one case, a student thought that the READ statement caused the values to be additive, and that repeated READ statements could yield a running total. This same error was detected in the Pascal study (Sleeman et al. 1986, 10) (It is likely that the students had no knowledge of the commands and were merely applying a literal interpretation of them. This misunderstanding may never happen with instructed students.)

In addition to the confusion students have with the use of the READ statement to assign values to variables, Putnam et al. (1986, 466) identified a series of control errors associated with the relationship between the READ statement and the DATA statement. Some suggested that when two READ commands with different variables were used, they acted independently and each accessed all the values in the DATA statements.

In programming, a variable must be viewed as a label, a label which corresponds to a particular location in memory and holds the value of the variable. The program or the programmer deliberately assigns the value to the location. Value assignment is a controlled operation, and even when the actual value assigned is generated at random, the assignment is done in a very explicit manner.

The research is clear: the one major difficulty for the beginning programmer is understanding the concept and implication of the use of variables in programs. An appreciation of variables requires a student be able to perform at Piaget's level of formal thought. An abstraction that requires a distinction between a fixed name and a changeable value takes time to assimilate. Even though students at the high school level can be expected to have reached the general stage of formal thought, it has been shown that when a learner encounters a new area of study he is inclined to revert back to an earlier level of development for cognitive strategies. Ausubel et al. (1978, 252) has suggested that even with mature learners, new subjects should be introduced at the concrete level. In the case of variables, the concept should be introduced with visualization, modeling, or analogies, rather than with reference to abstract mathematical processes which may or may not have been previously mastered by the learner.

Repetition

Surely one of the outstanding features of any computer is its ability to do repetitious tasks with precision and endurance. Babbage's original design of the computer was an effort to reduce certain mechanical mathematical calculations to routine operations which would not fall short because of human error (Augarten 1984, 40).

The key to repetition in a computer can be found in the control functions or commands built into a particular language. The implementation of these control functions may vary from language to language, but the general concept remains the same. The computer is instructed to do a particular segment of code repeatedly until a specific condition is met or while a condition holds. Somewhere within the code that is being repeated is a procedure which checks to see whether or not the condition is met.

Iteration. The simplest control command for repetition is the FOR/NEXT loop in BASIC. If the FOR and the NEXT are considered the boundaries of the repetition, then we need only look at what happens between them as the code that must be processed repeatedly until the condition is met. Within the syntax of the command structure we have the variables which fix the number of repetitions.

The statement FOR X = 1 TO 3 means that a series of commands will be executed starting with the variable X having a value of 1 and until the value of X exceeds 3. The value of X can be changed within the loop, but this can complicate the execution of the loop and it is generally considered a poor programming practice. The value of X is always changed at the end of the loop by the NEXT X statement. This statement does two things: it first increments the value of X by 1 (as in the statement LET X = X + 1) and then checks to see if X has exceeded the limit, in this case, 3. The NEXT statement is actually shorthand for two distinct steps. If this sounds confusing, it is only because it is confusing. It is difficult to describe clearly the process of a FOR/NEXT loop to someone unfamiliar with the subject. Beginning students do not have this knowledge.

Given the following program segment, it is helpful to use a line table, or a structured walkthrough, to show students what happens to the variables in a program as the program is executed.

```
100  FOR X = 1 TO 3
110  LET A = A + X
120  LET B = A + X
130  NEXT X
```

As tedious as it might be, working through a few examples using a line table can be very helpful in establishing the flow of a program through a FOR/NEXT loop. In working through a program segment involving repetition, it is important to focus on (1) the entry conditions for the loop, (2) checking for the exit condition, and (3) the values of the variables after the completion of the loop. It is important that the student understand the function of a simple loop before being confronted with nested loops or more complex control sequences.

Another problem students may have with the FOR/NEXT loop is not understanding when the control variable needs to be initialized for the loop. In the previous example, the value of X is set to 1 when line 100 is executed the first time; but each time through the loop, it is changed. What is different about the second and third time through the loop? One possible way of viewing this situation is to make it clear that line 100 can be reached under different conditions. In the first case, the line is called from somewhere outside the loop as part of a branch, or the line comes up in the normal sequence of line numbers. If this is the case, the line

Line Number	Value of X	Value of A	Value of B
ENTER LOOP			
100	1		
110	1	1	
120	1	1	2
130	2	1	2
100	2	1	2
110	2	3	2
120	2	3	5
130	3	3	5
100	3	3	5
110	3	6	5
120	3	6	9
130	4	6	9
EXIT LOOP			

Figure 2.3. Line Table for Simple FOR/NEXT Loop

can be thought of as being independent and the loop is initialized. Graphically this can be shown to students as:

```
              ||
              ||
              V
100   FOR X = 1 TO 3
110   LET A = A + X
120   LET B = A + X
130   NEXT X
```

When line 100 is called from within its own loop, it can be viewed as part of the loop, and is therefore not initialized. In the diagram that follows, (Fig. 2.4) a simple loop is broken down into five separate steps, some of which are repeated. The only one that is not repeated is STEP 1.

Teaching the related control functions such as DO/WHILE or IF/THEN/ELSE can be done in the same way.

An interesting and somewhat unexpected error involving loops was detected in both the BASIC (Putnam et al 1986, 467) and the Pascal (Sleeman et al. 1986, 591) studies of student errors. Some students had a tendency to include a PRINT or WRITELN

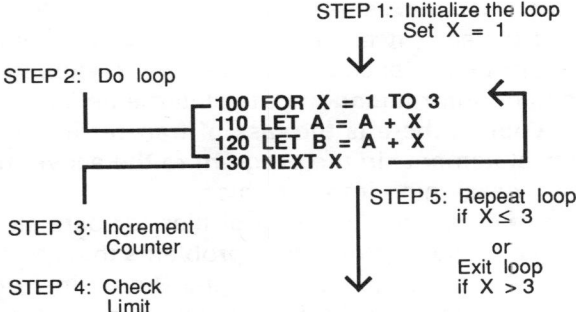

Figure 2.4. *Steps in the FOR/NEXT Loop.*

that immediately followed a loop into the scope of the loop. Obviously, students must be impressed with the notion that certain groups of statements define the limits of structures which control repetition. Mayer (1979, 591) suggests that certain groups of statements be viewed as "chunks" of code in order to make them distinct. Students may need to be taught to understand and write code in "chunks" that have a specific function (loops, for instance) rather than line by line.

Loops are troublesome because the naive programmer has to understand what is happening behind the scenes as the program progresses through the loop. Some students miss the point that a counter is being used and checked at some stage in the process, while others assume the process includes a constant check on all control conditions.

Recursion. Repetition can be accomplished through the utilization of subroutines. Some computer languages have the ability for subroutines to call themselves as a method of developing concise and elegant code. This feature is known as recursion. The concept will be discussed in the next chapter under structured programming.

Data Storage

Possibly the simplest concept in a program is the storage of information. It should be easy to explain to students that there are only two choices of location for information needed to the operate of a program. The first storage location is within the program itself, the second is in independent files which are used in conjunction with the program.

The former case makes use of the DATA and READ statement in BASIC and typically it presents little conceptual difficulty for students, except that a teacher must be sure to explain the problems of changing information in data statements from within the program. Of course, there is the task of transferring information from the data statements in the program to the active memory of the program by assigning it to variables.

The second case, the utilization of files for data storage, can present a whole range of problems—problems that are somewhat dependent on the language being taught. But an instructor must first establish the idea that the information is stored on the disk and not in the computer memory, before getting involved in the complexities of syntax in a particular language or dialect.

There is no research on problems encountered by novices when dealing with files, but this is probably because the teaching about files is not part of introductory courses on programming. This is unfortunate, because almost any application of significance requires the use of files.

The problem with files is that the learner does not have direct access to the information on the disk. Students can get a listing of their program, but they cannot "see" the information on the disk. In the debugging operation, a student has to consider several possibilities: that the information on the disk is not what he thinks it is, or that the information is there but in some unknown format, or that the process that he is using to read the information is at fault.

Experience has shown that students can be introduced to files more effectively if the procedure is highly structured. To begin with, the structure of the data needs to be firmly established. Starting with a sequential file, this concept can be introduced by having the students write a program that reads information—a list of student names, for example—from DATA statements and prints them out to the screen in the sequence read and in the reverse order. To avoid confusion, and to limit typing errors, the DATA statements are provided to the students on disk. The student knows that the data is correct, and he can see it on the screen or in his/her program listing. Obviously, the student would need to read the data into memory using a loop, and then print it out using another loop or loops. The students are told not to proceed until they can accomplish this part of the task.

The students are then shown how the code should be changed in order to read from a sequential file which would contain the identical data in a sequential format. Again the data, in the form of a file, is provided to insure the students that they do indeed have the correct information on the disk. It must be emphasized that the data in a sequential file on the disk is in the same format as the data in the DATA statements in the program.

Writing to a file is delayed until the students are confident that they can read information from a file on disk. The instruction can be supplemented by using a sector editor to examine the data on the disk, and viewing the data on the screen using an operating system command.

Just as a student needs to have some idea about the operations that take place within a computer when it is processing data, a student should also understand the procedure of exchanging data with a file.

The teaching of random access files would follow a similar pattern, with the student being provided with a sample file on disk and then being taught how to read it before being asked to write to a random access file. Once a student can read from a random access file, writing to a file is not all that difficult. That is not to say complications do not exist due to records overriding records, but beginning students can learn both types of files. It is helpful to supply students with printed copies of disk sectors containing sequential files and random access files for comparison purposes. A printout of a sector from a disk with a list of names in a sequential file might be compared to a printout of a sector with the same list of names in a random access file.

Alphanumeric Characters

String Manipulation. The manipulation of strings is one aspect of programming that is interesting to students. It gives students an opportunity to test their creative skills without becoming overly involved in computation. One of the reasons that this aspect of programming is so generally liked by students is that they can see the direct results of their work.

Some typical assignments might be:

1. Ask a person to input his full name, first name first, and then have it printed to the screen in the reverse order.
2. Have someone input a name, and have it written repeatedly until it covers the entire screen.
3. Ask a person to input a name and have it snake its way around the edge of the screen.

4. Ask a user to type in their name, and then have it shown on the screen in the reverse order.

If there is a problem with strings, it is making the learner aware that numerals stored as alphanumeric strings are not the same as numbers stored as numeric variables. This might best be accomplished by focusing on the difference in the naming of the types of variables, and the process of storing and recovering the variables from their separate locations in memory. If the house analogy is used, it should be made clear that the strings stored in the "houses" can be any ASCII characters and are not limited to letters.

String Conversion. Once it is firmly established that there is a difference between alphanumeric and numeric strings, the next step is to consider the conversion of one type of variable to the other. Here again the process is as important to a student's understanding as the syntax. When the value of variable X is converted to the value of variable X$, the student should know that the computer goes through a series of steps to make the conversion:

1. The computer goes to the memory locations allocated to X and takes the value of the variable and places it somewhere in the CPU. The value stored at original memory locations does not change.
2. The value placed in the CPU is processed by means of a fixed set of steps into its string counterpart. The string counterpart is a completely different set of bits and bytes.
3. The string counterpart is then placed in the memory locations allocated to X$.

The conversion that takes place in the CPU is unimportant to the programmer, but it is important for the programmer to know that at the end of the process he has two variables, each containing equivalent information, but radically different in terms of bits and bytes. The conversion of a number to a string does not change the number.

It would be nice if the reverse process was also true. Does the conversion of a string into a number leave both memory locations with the same information? A quick analysis would show this is not always the case. When a string is converted to a number, the process is slightly different.

1. The computer goes to the memory locations allocated to X$ and takes the value of the variable and places it somewhere in the CPU. The value stored at memory locations designated for X$ does not change.
2. The value placed in the CPU is processed by means of a fixed set of steps into its numeric counterpart. If the string has a numeric counterpart, it is assigned to X. If it does not have a numeric counterpart than most systems will assign the value of O to the numeric variable. In either case, the numeric counterpart is a completely different set of bits and bytes.
3. The numeric counterpart is then placed in the memory locations allocated to X.

At the end of this process, X$ still has its original value, and X has the numeric counterpart to X$, but the information may not be equivalent in both locations. If a student understands why the two processes are not reciprocal, he understands the concept of string conversion.

Number Manipulation

The computational abilities of computers are of themselves easy to understand, if the computations are understood by the programmer. On the other hand, having access to powerful computational algorithms means very little, if the programmer does not have at least an intuitive sense of what is being done.

A teacher should know what quantitative skills and mathematics concepts his/her students understand in order to teach them to use the computational powers of the computer effectively. Something as simple as the priority of operations can be unintelligible to a student who does not appreciate the role that parentheses play in the case of arithmetical algorithms. The question is whether students need to become involved in mathematical problems that exceed minimum operations in an introductory programming course.

Computation. Certainly, at the high school level, students should be expected to understand the basic operations of addition, subtraction, multiplication and division. The use of the * to represent multiplication and the / for division are not problems once they are presented, except that the function of the same characters within a PRINT statement can cause some confusion.

It must be made clear that any character or symbol presented as part of a character string in a PRINT command is not executable. This should be done before the topic of computation is taken up.

As a start, the LET command can be used as the main command for the purpose of calculations. Students have little problem with the notion that whatever computation is indicated to the right of the replace (=) sign is done and the answer is stored in the memory location specified at the left. It may be necessary to step through an example or two of some simple computations to show how the process is done. The problems demonstrated should be simple and not involve issues of priorities of operation.

A similar sequence of instructions might use the computational aspects of the PRINT command. It should be noted at this point that although the two commands lead to the same numeric results, there is an essential difference in the process because when the PRINT command is used for computational purposes, the results of the computation are not stored in memory. The design of a program might determine which command is more efficient.

Operational Priority. Students are typically not aware that the sequence of calculations can affect the final answer. If a course is going to involve any significant calculations, then the students will need to know this before they develop their own algorithms. The necessity for an order of operations can easily be demonstrated, but it is unlikely that the students will appreciate the necessity for such detail until they encounter it in their own programming.

A teacher should anticipate the level of need that his/her students might have, and provide them with sufficient drill and practice to make them cautious in developing their own algorithms, or recognize the problem quickly in the debugging stage.

Functions. The use of functions in a program presents a more serious problem. Often students do not have an appreciation of the concept of a function, and it is a concept, like the notion of a variable, that cannot be quickly taught. It may be that by dealing with functions on a computer, a student will gain some insight into their operations. In the not-too-distant past, the only way to handle certain trigonometric functions was to use a table in the back of a book, look up a value in the appropriate column and row, and substitute the value in the equation in place of the function. Learning this aspect of trigonometry was one of following a table-search algorithm which had no connection to the problem under consideration. The process sometimes reduced the exercises to meaningless memorization of a set of search directions, with little or no

understanding of the mathematical concepts or geometric interpretation.

Although the computer may not be a solution to the problem,
it does remove the need to insert a table-search between the question and the answer. The use of resident functions can bring students closer to a problem than table-searches.

It might seem that the concept of a function need not be addressed in an introductory course, but in fact it might be one of
the concepts that a student will encounter when he uses applications software. In order to get the most out of a spread sheet or a
data base, a user must be able to use the built-in functions. For
example, in a spreadsheet, a user should understand that the SUM
function can total a line or a column of data, and the user should
understand what is going on when he selects the function from a
list.

Usually, the functions in an introductory courses are less complex than those in applications programs. The square root function
might be an example. In this case the function would require a
single operand which may be a constant or a variable.

The concept the student needs is that for every value of an
operand, a function will provide a corresponding value within
whatever limits are required by the function. The computer relieves
the user of going through the steps to determine the value; the
programmer is not concerned about this process, but he does need
to know that a value will be generated. With the possible exception
of matrix functions (which are often not available on microcomputers), the functions that are available tend to generate a single
numeric value.

Information Exchange

In addition to the information stored in a program in the form
of DATA statements, and the information available to a program
from files, a computer can receive and send information back and
forth to a user. One of the features of BASIC is to provide real-
time interaction with a user—real-time as compared to batch. One
of the reasons that BASIC continues to be a popular language for
introductory courses is that it allows for real-time programs and
often makes available an immediate mode.

Input. Keyboard interaction can be achieved through the IN-
PUT command. This is the simplest and most direct process. What
the novice programmer should know is that if the information is

requested of the user, the program needs to receive the information and store it in memory as a variable. This is done in a straightforward way without any "discretion" on the part of the computer. If the user is asked to input an even number, the computer will accept any number. The INPUT command has no way of evaluating the input to see that it is indeed an even number.

The INPUT command is an unconditional command which relies on the user for data in the appropriate form. That is not to say data for input cannot be checked to see that it is appropriate, but the input command itself has little to do with it.

Output. The computer's ability to output information to a user is slightly more complex, but not much. The difference is that the computer has two or more options. It can send the information to the screen or to a printer. In a user-friendly program, the choice is often left to the user.

Although the input and output functions of a computer are conceptually easy to understand, the practice of producing data in user-friendly format can be a very time-consuming task. Formatting screens and reports can be a major aspect of any software development project.

When the output from the program is sent to a disk or other storage device, the syntax is more complicated, but for the most part the concepts are similar to sending data to a printer. With some languages and dialects of BASIC, the file commands are simple and create no learning problems; unfortunately this is not the case with the popular Microsoft BASIC.

Subroutines

The introduction of the idea of a subroutine often becomes far more complex than necessary. An introduction to the concept might follow a rationale that if certain segments of code are used more than once in a program it would be more efficient if the code could be reused rather than being entered several times at different places in the program. Students certainly appreciate saving time inputting the program.

Subroutines can be linked to the concept of a function. If students have already been exposed to the use of functions, then the subroutine can be taught as if it were a form of user-defined function. At the machine level this is very nearly true, the only significant difference being that functions generally have specified parameters, while subroutines tend to use global variables.

The placement of subroutines within the program may present some problems unless the students are taught early that they need to plan ahead. Subroutines should be placed outside the main program to isolate them from the execution of the main program. As mentioned earlier, some teachers place the subroutines at the beginning of the program because it has been shown to make the running of a program more efficient. However, it can be argued that such placement destroys the logical flow of the program for the beginning student, and if that is the case, the efficiency gained in execution of a program is frequently lost in the inefficiency of reading and interpreting the code. If the program is compiled rather than interpreted, a time-saving is not achieved.

The debate on placement really should take into account whether a program is being prepared for an interpreted or a compiled language, but it is essential that the subroutines not be placed within the main body of the program. Actually the primary concern should be clarity of design and not efficiency of operation.

More important in the learning considerations, subroutines must be contrasted with functions, both those available in the language and those that can be user defined. The contrast might include not only the syntactical considerations but the machine-level operation as well. The purpose of this discussion is to draw the student's attention to the similarities and differences in these closely related aspects of programming.

Nesting. In a curriculum based on modules and structured programming, the idea that subroutines can be called from other subroutines should not present any conceptual difficulties. If the subroutines are isolated as separate units, and if they they are limited to performing single functions, then the power of structured programming should be manifested in that students will be able to comprehend the logic and power of nesting of subroutines.

It may be necessary to point out limitations in some languages with regard to the level of nesting of subroutines. These limitations are ordinarily not encountered in an introductory course unless the student makes an error in design which results in a subroutine being somehow embedded in a loop. Typically in a microcomputer a stack of limited size stores the CPU parameters that are needed when control is returned from a subroutine to the calling location.

The ability to have a subroutine call itself is not available in all versions of all languages. As mentioned under repetition, this property is called recursion, and it is a powerful tool for certain numeric and geometric problems, but it does require that the operating system have a process for handling repeated calls to the same subroutine. Recursion will be discussed in more detail under structured programming.

Argument Passing. One of the characteristics of Microsoft BASIC is that all variables are global. Within a program there is one and only one memory location that corresponds to a particular variable, and at any time in the execution of the program there is only a single value that this location can hold. This seems only fair. If a variable can have more than one value, how would the programmer ever keep track of what was going on in a program.

The problem that arises out of this is that the programmer must be sure that he does not use the same name for more than one variable. In a large program this can be troublesome, and it is particularly troublesome when a program is done in modules by different programmers. It is not uncommon for different segments of a program to use the same variable name for different variables. Of all the reasons given for BASIC not being taken seriously as a programming language the fact that most versions are restricted to global variables is the most compelling.

Pascal, on the other hand, is typically written so that all variables are local, and their names are restricted to the particular module in which they are defined. Because of this, each module or subroutine can be viewed as an independent unit. Values for variables can be passed as parameters for the modules or subroutines, and they need not be identified by the same variable name. When necessary, Pascal does allow for the assignment of values to global variables. Local and global variables are an integral part of Pascal, and they are one of the compelling reasons for Pascal being a favorite language for proponents of structured programming.

Arrays

Surely one of the most mystifying aspects of programming to the novice is the concept of an array. The reason for this is not clear; it could be just the result of poor instruction. If the instruction is not better than the explanations provided in most textbooks on programming, then instructors are probably to blame.

The problem begins with the use of the term "array." At best it is a meaningless term, at worst it carries with it the mathematical context of matrix algebra. In either case, the term itself is not very useful to the novice programmer.

The first step in developing the concept of arrays is to present the idea that it is possible to establish lists of variables in a computer. The idea of a list is easy to imagine. Students can see that having a list of names or numbers identified as a separate part of memory makes sense, and certainly is better than having to create a separate, specific variable name for each entry in the list. Syntax is avoided until the idea that computer memories can hold such lists in an efficient and orderly way has been grasped. The first step in the transition is to make it clear that each value stored in the list can be identified by a name that represents the portion of memory where the list is stored. Then introducing the idea that the particular variable can be identified by its number in the list. It almost seems too simple.

The same approach can be used for two-dimensional arrays, except the anchoring concept is a table rather than a list, and two numbers are needed to identify a particular location in the table. Some teachers prefer to use the idea of rooms in a building which have to be identified by a floor number and a room number, but this method may conjure up undue complications because the building analogy requires the student to think about an unusual type of building with uniform floors and rooms. In any case, teachers should be cautioned that students cannot be taught two-dimensional arrays until they are comfortable with the one-dimensional array, and this is a lengthy processes.

Other forms of data structures do not typically come up in introductory courses. They should not be introduced until the student is comfortable with arrays, and a need can be demonstrated for situations in which the simple array approach is not adequate either because of the form of the data or the efficiency of the processes using the data.

APPLICATIONS CONCEPTS

It is not the purpose of this text to consider all possible instruction that might be part of the curriculum concerning computers. For our purposes, computer science is viewed as being primarily the arena of programming and software development. Be that as it may, many high school computer science teachers are called upon to teach courses concerned with the general use of the computer as a tool. In some schools, computer science courses focus on computer applications rather than programming.

A distinction can be made between courses that are based on programming and those based on applications software in terms of the types of problem solving that are involved. Programming courses are more likely to involve general problem-solving skills such as breaking a program down into parts, identification of variables, etc.; whereas courses built around applications software tend to focus on developing specific skills in word processing or the use of spreadsheets.

Consequently, the choice of applications software is more important than choosing a programming language for novices. The novice programmer is expected to move on to other languages as he gains skill, but the applications user is more likely to use the package that he is introduced to in the first place. The teaching of applications software should be done with the most up-to-date package available and affordable. Producers of software are alert to this phenomenon and are providing inexpensive versions of their software to establish themselves in the school environment.

Teachers of applications software should recognize that they can be trapped into teaching highly specific skills, and fail to give proper attention to overriding concepts. The teaching of applications software can become similar to teaching the syntax of a language without drawing out general ideas and concepts. Almost every applications package requires knowledge of specific functions—system setup, data input, editing, storage, and output. The manner in which a particular system manages these functions is probably useful and necessary information if the learner is going to be able to transfer the knowledge learned using one package to another. There is little, if any, research on the ability of students to transfer knowledge between applications packages, although it is almost certain that such transfer is possible, and that some instructional procedures may be more effective in promoting this transfer.

In addition to cost and availability, three considerations should be made in selecting applications software: friendliness, compatibility and capacity.

Friendliness

Teaching applications software has come a long way from the early days when the only package available was AppleWriter on the Apple II +. Control keys were needed for every command, and lower case was not available on the screen, but was available for printout. What was seen on the screen was a long way from what was obtained in the printout. Enthusiasm was high, but motivation was necessary to conquer the secrets that linked the software to the printers. It was not a simple thing to introduce someone to the efficiencies of word processing.

Fortunately, the situation has changed, and "user-friendly" software is available for almost any combination of hardware. It is unnecessary to tell a student that he needs to remember to double strike the escape key to get a capital letter or that an escape, control-B might yield bold print. The "what you see is what you get" approach coupled with pull-down menus, help screens, and icons has made many software packages much easier to use in the classroom.

With more and more user-friendly features in software, less time should be necessary for mechanics and more time can be given to general ideas or processes. Teachers of applications software have to be alert to the potential of teaching about the similarities and differences between packages rather than just inputting and revising data.

Compatibility

Every effort should be made to use a consistent set of software in instruction. Compatible or integrated packages seem to be the most reasonable approach when they are available. At one time it was necessary to learn a specific set of control keys for a word processor, and another for a spreadsheet, and yet a third for a database. The time wasted in the process, let alone the time lost by using a wrong sequence, has led many novices to the conclusion that the whole idea of saving time with a computer is a myth.

Compatibility must also extend into the workplace for those students who are taking an applications course with the intent of applying the skills acquired. These students not only require compatible software that is internally consistent, but they must have software compatible with those presently in use in the outside world. This is a problem that might better be addressed in the business education departments of high schools where administrators must ensure currently acceptable, marketable skills.

Instruction in applications software with the intent of providing entry-level skills can be very expensive. Not only must the software be revised on a regular basis, but hardware in the workplace also changes frequently.

Capacity

Students need to understand that different application programs have significantly different capacities. Although the increase in available memory and storage capabilities of most microcomputer systems has reduced the need to trade off size of databases against functions, differences between applications programs remain. It was not too long ago that a database might lack the ability to sort more than one field, or could not be programmed to print mailing labels. Some very popular databases had record lengths limited to 256 characters.

Again, the teaching of applications software has to extend beyond the particular software used for instruction. Among the characteristics to be compared and contrasted are: the maximum document size for a word processor, the number of records in a database, or the number of columns and rows in a spreadsheet.

RECOMMENDED READINGS

Roy D. Pea, "Language-Independent Conceptual 'Bugs' in Novice Programming." Journal of Educational Computing Research, Vol. 2, No. 1, 1986, pp. 25–36. An excellent discussion of the errors that novices frequently make in programming, and how these might be viewed as being classifiable into three classes of "bugs." It is suggested that by understanding certain tendencies of novice programmers, teachers of programming might be more explicit in their instruction and reduce some of the frustrations encountered by beginners.

Richard E. Clark, "Confounding in Educational Computing Research." *Journal of Educational Computing Research*, Vol. 1, No. 2, 1985, pp. 137–148. A sobering criticism of the research on computer-based instruction which raises serious questions concerning the reported effectiveness of computer-aided instruction (CAI). In part, he suggests that the research fails to explore the unique qualities of the computer in the educational setting, and that many of the reported effects may lack content validity due to the fact that the computer is not a uniform medium and the motivational effects of the novelty of the medium may be more significant factors than the independent variables studies. Although the focus of the article is on CAI, the confounding variables are operational during research on the effectiveness of programming.

Ralph T. Putnam, D. Sleeman, Juliet A. Baxter, and Laiani K. Kuspa, "A Summary of Misconceptions of High School BASIC Programmers." *Journal of Educational Computing Research*, Vol 2, No. 4, 1986, p. 459–472. One of the most thorough studies of students' understandings of the syntax of BASIC and Pascal. It shows some consistency across languages and provide useful classification of errors.

D. Sleeman, Ralph T. Putnam, Juliet A. Baxter, and Laiani K. Kuspa, "Pascal and High School Students: A Study of Errors." *Journal of Educational Computing Research*, Vol. 2, No. 1, 1986, pp. 5–23. One of the most thorough studies of students' understandings of the syntax of BASIC and Pascal. It shows some consistency across languages and provide useful classification of errors.

Benedict Du Boulay, "Some Difficulties of Learning To Program." *Journal of Educational Computing Research*, Vol. 2, No. 1, 1986, pp. 57–73. An examination of some of the conceptual problems that novice programmers face. In addition to problems of syntax, he suggests that there are four other areas of difficulty: orientation, the notional machine, structures, and pragmatics.

SUGGESTED ACTIVITIES

1. Interview no less than four students who are completing or have completed their first course in BASIC programming, and ask them to explain what is happening inside a computer with the following commands:

LET A = B + 1	PRINT C
LET D = 0	PRINT "C"
IF A < B GOTO 99	INPUT A
20 DATA 80, 90, 99	30 READ A
60 GOTO 30	

If ERIC documents are available to you, check your results with Pirays Bayman and Richard E. Mayer, *Novice User's Misconceptions of BASIC Programming Statements*. Report No. 82-1, California University, SantaBarbara, CA, 1982, ED 238395

2. Select three of the common errors made by novice pro-

grammers that have been described in this chapter, or in the research referenced, and write a diagnostic test item(s) that could be used to distinguish between those students who have each of the misconceptions and those that do not. Include with the test item(s) a clear identification of the error under study.

3. Prepare three program segments which are executable but result in an error in printout due to one of each of the following types of errors: syntax, sequence, or context. Include the proper program segment to demonstrate the intended printout.

4. Write a program that asks a user for his name and then takes the name and moves it, like a snake, around the screen starting in the upper left-hand corner. Corners should be smoothly turned one letter at a time.

5. Prepare two programs, one that will write a ten-name list to a disk in a sequential file, and the other which will write the same list of names into a random access file. Using a sector editor, locate and print out the sector(s) on the disk that contain the two files. Label the two printouts and incorporate the two program segments on the printouts so as to provide a student handout showing the difference in the data storage.

6. Prepare a set of visuals for the overhead projector that demonstrate the need for operational priority when dealing with arithmetical functions.

CHAPTER 3
ELEMENTS OF STRUCTURED PROGRAMMING

If there is anything that computer science professionals agree upon, it is that programming must be structured. This premise is so fundamental to the discipline of computer science that there are no detractors. Unfortunately, the term is invoked in almost the same way that "computer literacy" has been invoked by the education community. It is used as if everyone knew exactly what is meant, and yet the term has no operational definition. The confusion is most apparent at the high school level where the teachers are often self-taught, with limited knowledge of programming syntax and probably no training in software development and engineering.

The experienced high school teacher is aware of the problems associated with undisciplined programming. He hears that he must teach students structured programming, but a clear image of what this means and what criteria might be applied to define the concept has not been presented. For some, the concept merely means that a structured program has the code organized in a consistent way; others have extended the concept to include the use of a main menu or module which controls a series of subroutines. These characteristics, organization and subroutines, are certainly critical criteria for structured programs, but structured programming includes much more.

Most high school teachers are limited to a form of Microsoft BASIC for teaching programming. Microsoft BASIC is not conducive to disciplined programming. There are ample examples of structured programming being taught using BASIC, but the common dialects do not help foster a reliance on program algorithms which consistently apply the same series of steps or decision rules to control the flow of the program. When such control structures are part of the syntax of the languages, they can provide for efficient implementation and better internal documentation. Lacking

53

the internal structure, BASIC programmers frequently resort to less formal algorithms.

Some have tried to offset this by going to a structured language, but the most readily available procedural language for the microcomputer is LOGO. Many teachers have trouble taking LOGO seriously as an authentic programming language. It would be better for the high school teacher if the language was not touted so strongly as a language for primary-age children.

In any case, what high school teachers of computer science must understand is that whatever language they work with, computer science is evolving as a well-defined discipline with its own protocols and procedures. These can be taught at any level and with any language, but first the teacher must know and appreciate the structure of the discipline.

This is not an attempt to place responsibility for the sad state of affairs in the teaching of introductory programming on the shoulders of high school teachers. This is an evolving discipline, and knowledge still flows along informal channels. Although some of the most outstanding advocates of structured programming are professors of computer science, much of the development is taking place in the "real world" of commercial data processing and software development. The practicing high school teacher has no direct contact with either of these areas; in fact, the professionals in college and industry are having difficulty developing their own networks.

Many college instructors are having the same problems in teaching as their high school counterparts. They tend to teach as they have been taught, and the tradition in computer science instruction is to teach the mechanics of syntax and operating systems without giving high priority to planning, style, and maintenance.

This chapter is designed as a primer on the concepts and procedures of structured programming. From the developing literature of the discipline, those elements of style and process have been chosen that might be most helpful in designing and teaching a beginning programming course. It should be noted that no particular language is used, and as far as possible, examples are language-free.

HISTORY

Most computer scientists agree that the beginnings of structured programming can be traced to Edsger Dijkstra's 1965 article

"Programming Considered as a Human Activity." It was obvious to Dijkstra that information had to be grouped and organized into manageable structures, and that the development of programs would be more efficient if the design followed mathematical principles or guidelines. He pointed out that programmers must give at least as much attention to "elegance" of design as they were giving to efficient use of computer core and computer time.

At the time, programs were becoming more and more complex, and programmers were beginning to spend more time correcting and updating than they were generating new code. The biggest problem was that programmers updating other programmers' code had difficulty following the original logic. The program itself had to be considered in the light of good engineering design principles.

If there was a single recommendation that most affected programming, it was a letter from Dijkstra to the Association for Computing Machinery. (1968) He argued strongly against the unconditional jump—the GOTO command—because it made the logic of a program difficult to follow and analyze. He argued for the reliance on just three control structures; simple sequencing, alternation, and repetition. In essence, his guiding principles of structured programming have evolved into a few simple concepts: (1) a program is a set of modules, (2) each module performs a single function, and (3) the program is organized into a hierarchical structure which shows the logical connection between the modules.

In order to provide an instructional environment that would follow the guidelines for structured programming, Niklaus Wirth developed a new language: Pascal. It has become the language of choice in most academic programs because of (1) its structured procedural format, (2) its requirement of declared variables, and (3) its ability to handle local and global variables. These same characteristics made Pascal a popular language among software developers.

Although Pascal was developed as an instructional language, it was geared to the college not the high school environment, for students interested in programming careers rather than merely in becoming computer literate. Pascal is a formal language with many artificial rules and an inflexible grammar and syntax. It is not as close to being a natural language as BASIC, and it may not serve the purpose of the general high school curriculum. BASIC comes very close to being a spoken language, Pascal does not. Pascal's acceptance as the language of choice in the high school is also hampered by its cost and the lack of instructors trained to teach it.

Pascal does have a role in the high school curriculum. The language was "established" in 1983 when the College Entrance Examination Board designated Pascal as the official language for its advanced placement examination. The consensus among computer scientists is that structured programming is essential. In addition, many computer science educators feel that a student taught structuring processes and principles will develop problem-solving skills in addition to learning a set of rules and procedures. The role of Pascal and BASIC will be part of a continuing debate for the foreseeable future, and there will surely be those who will argue for LOGO, LISP, and other languages as curriculum needs become clearer.

Historically, the trend to structured programming has proceeded through a transition from completely unstructured and undisciplined programming to what is becoming highly stylized and controlled. The conceptual development of structured programming can be illustrated by a series of diagrams.

Early programming was designed to solve specific problems, typically involving extensive computations. Every effort was expended to make the programs run as efficiently as possible because of the high cost of operating a mainframe computer. The shorter

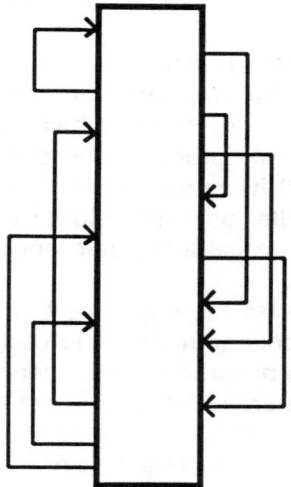

Figure 3.1. Spaghetti Code

the program, the more efficient. The tendency was to re-use as much code as possible. Figure 3.1 shows a program written by an efficient programmer who used extensive unconditional branching. This is sometimes referred to as "spaghetti code". The problem with spaghetti code is that it can be unintelligible to other programmers, and at times even to the original programmer who may lose the logic that seemed so evident when it was first written.

As long as a program remains short and is restricted to simple applications or problems, spaghetti code may work; but this style leads to unmanageable programs, and once the length of the program exceeds a hundred lines, even the hardiest "hacker" soon learns that some order or flow is necessary.

The second level is a linear paradigm with few if any unconditional branches. This might be symbolized by the diagram in Figure 3.2. This is obviously an oversimplification, because it is unlikely that any program that performs a useful function would be so linear, but it is a guide or goal for a programmer. A programmer using subroutines, duplicating program segments, and avoiding novel coding could take an undisciplined spaghetti-type segment and bring it closer to the linear form shown in Figure 3.2. What is lost in economy of code is made up for in flexibility and ease of maintenance.

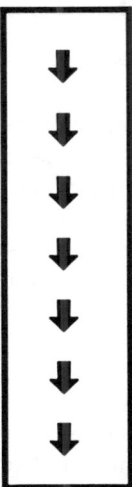

Figure 3.2. Linear Code

The linear model was improved by the practice of breaking the program down into segments that separate the program into functional parts, as illustrated in Figure 3.3. The execution of the program was then conceptualized as a flow from one part or segment to the next. A program was viewed as a simple sequence of events. Repetition was handled within segments, and, when appropriate, repeated functions were handled through the use of subroutines.

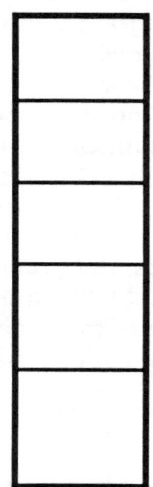

Figure 3.3. Segmented Linear Code

Next in the development of programming models, the segments are separated into independent blocks or modules, as shown in Figure 3.4. The difference here is that the modules are independent and self-contained. Again, with appropriate consideration for subroutines, the concept was that the flow of the program passed from one module to the next in sequence, following a well-designed pattern.

The final model in the developmental sequence is the structured, top-down format shown in Figure 3.5. This represents the goal of this chapter: to understand the rationale, rules and guidelines for the development of top-down, structured programs. At the top of the structure is the most general module, and the flow goes down the structure with each level increasing in specificity. The flow is always top to bottom.

Figure 3.4. Modular Code

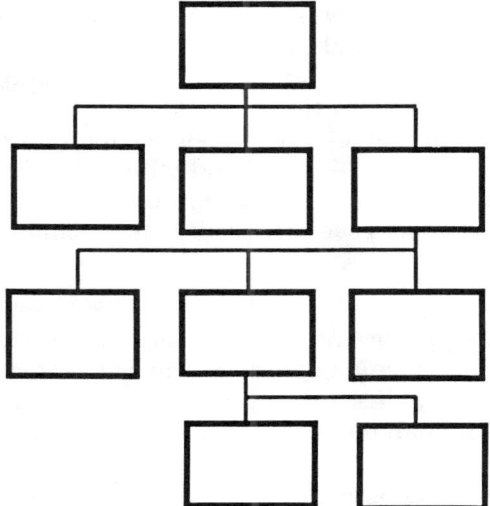

Figure 3.5. Top-Down Structure

OBJECTIVES

Having a structured program is not an end in itself. The arguments in favor of structured programs stem from the need to develop clear and concise code that will produce programs that will run. The rationale is that if more time is spent in planning and organizing a program, less time will be spent in modifying and adapting it. A significant portion of the development stage of a program should be spent considering future modifications. Systematic structured programming should lead to easier program maintenance.

To be very specific, the goals of structured programming are:

1. To produce programs that will run and meet specifications on their first trial.
2. To produce programs that are easily modified and maintained.

A structured program has two important advantages. Not only does it provide for better maintenance, but it makes the whole software development process more efficient. In some applications, a library of procedures may be developed to the point that the creation of a program would require little more than the writing of a master menu or module which would rely on the library.

The goals for teaching structured programming are not necessarily the same as those for using structuring techniques in the commercial environment, but the qualities of organization, clarity, and efficiency—the qualities of good structured programming—are at the basis of any systematic approach to problem solving. The following elements seem to justify the teaching of structured programming:

1. Structured programming is the best and most realistic approach for teaching computer science as it is practiced.
2. Students who learn structured programming will not have to unlearn material that they might learn in a nonstructured approach.
3. The same elements that add clarity to structured programs can add clarity to instruction.

This final point may outweigh all the others, from the teacher's point of view.

In this chapter, the process of developing structured programs will be discussed from the viewpoint of instructional use. As part of the presentation, the structured flowcharts proposed by Nassi and Shneiderman (1973) will be used. They have suggested that certain diagrams become the building blocks for modules. Six of the basic blocks are shown in Figure 3.6. Detailed information on these types of diagrams will be presented later in the chapter.

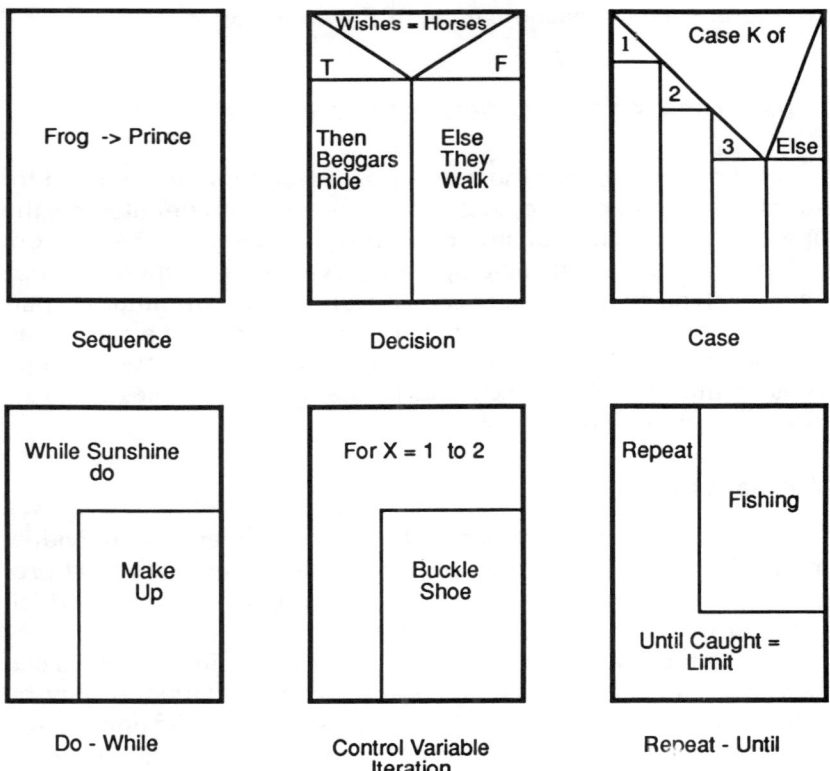

Figure 3.6. Structured Flowchart Building Blocks (Ralston and Reilly 1983)

These diagrams are referred to as iteration diagrams or by the names of their authors—Nassi-Shneiderman diagrams. The diagrams are a helpful visual technique for explaining structures, and students can be taught to use these diagrams as part of their documentation. Weiland (1983) has suggested that they replace traditional flowcharting when a more structured approach is used. Woodward (1987) suggests that the Nassi-Shneiderman diagrams can be helpful to introduce notions of modular, top-down design, pseudocoding and structured programming. They serve as tools for teaching and software development.

At the risk of repeating known material, the information will be presented as if it is essentially new material to the reader. In part this is done because of the limited access that most high school computer science teachers have to the source materials.

PRINCIPLES OF STRUCTURED PROGRAMMING

Although there is almost universal agreement on the need for structured programming, just as there is for computer literacy, the operational definition of structured programming is subject to on-going discussion and development. Over time, certain features have evolved that characterize structured programming. Of particular interest are those characteristics that might be part of an introductory course: modules, invocation, and top-down design. These features will be discussed as the basic principles of structured programming.

Modularity

The building blocks of a structured program are the individual modules of code which are linked together to form the total program. A module is a discrete set of programming statements which together perform a single logical function.

At the top level of abstraction of program design, modules can be viewed as black boxes which need to be understood only by what they do (function), what they need to do their job (input), and what results they produce (output). A program can be written at this level using "dummy" modules to show how the pieces of a program fit together.

At some point the actual code for the module has to be considered. Keep in mind that in planning the overall program, modules can be considered black boxes. However, as mentioned in Chapter 2, there is ample evidence that students require some visualization of the internal processes of a computer in order to have a meaningful understanding of programming statements.

Aside from being an independent unit, one characteristic of a module that requires special consideration is that a module should have one unique entry point and one unique exit point. The module itself is a self-contained, closed unit designed to perform one logical function.

Writing modules that follow the rules of being independent, discrete, closed, and performing a single logical function leads to more clarity in reading code, but it sometimes leads to a style that takes getting used to. For example, there might be a module in the form of a subroutine which searches a list (LIST(X)) of known length (LL) for a particular name (NAME$), and then prints the location of the name in the list (X). This might be written as:

```
940   REM
950   REM  ****************************
960   REM MODULE FOR LOCATING
970   REM THE POSITION OF A NAME
980   REM IN A LIST
990   REM  ****************************
995   REM
1000  FOR X = 1 TO LL
1010  IF LIST(X) = NAME$ THEN
      PRINT X: RETURN
1020  NEXT X
1030  PRINT "NAME NOT FOUND
      ON LIST."
1040  RETURN
```

This module has two exit points; one in line 1010 under the condition LIST(X) = NAME$, the other in line 1040. The alternative to this is the following module:

```
940   REM
950   REM  ****************************
960   REM MODULE FOR LOCATING
970   REM THE POSITION OF A NAME
980   REM IN A LIST
990   REM  ****************************
```

```
995    REM
1000   FOR X = 1 TO LL
1010   IF LIST(X) = NAME$ THEN
       PRINT X: LET X = LL:
       GOTO 1040
1020   NEXT X
1030   PRINT "NAME NOT FOUND
       ON LIST."
1040   RETURN
```

The entry point is always at line 1000, and the exit point is always at line 1040, and the value of X when the routine is completed is always equal to LL. The difference in the clarity of these two segments may not be apparent because of the simplicity of the function performed by the module, but as modules become more complex, the style becomes more helpful. (Note the use of the GOTO command in line 1010. The use of GOTOs are permitted by most structured programmers provided that the branching is within the module; some purists will disagree.)

In addition to the entry and exit condition, modules should be simple enough to be readily analyzed. One measure of the complexity of a program is the size of the modules; a minimum module size is desired. The size of a module should be limited for the convenience of the reader. In one of its manuals, IBM recommends that a program module not exceed 50 lines of code. (Walston and Felix 1977) This limit was determined by the number of lines of code that might conveniently be printed on a single page.

When the reader will be using a monitor screen, a good rule is that the number of lines should be limited to the number of lines on the screen. This means that the size of the module would be somewhere in the neighborhood of 20 to 30 lines for a program that will run on a microcomputer. The size limit for a module needs to be fixed through consideration of the programmer's working environment.

Another significant aspect of modules is that the number of types of functions that a module might perform is limited to three generic control functions—action, loop, or branch. These control functions need special attention, but before proceeding, the following criteria are offered for evaluating modules:

1. They should be independent of other modules.
2. They should perform a single logical function.

3. They should be discrete segments of code, clearly identifiable within the context of the program.
4. They should be closed segments with one entry point and one exit point.
5. They should have a limited number of lines of code as determined by the work environment.

Following these guidelines or characteristics should lead to code which is clear, flexible, and functional. Aside from the obvious advantages of clarity, well-structured modules have advantages over more traditional programming styles. Martin and McClure (1979) have summarized the advantages as follows:

1. If the function of a module changes, only that module changes and the rest of the program is unaffected.
2. If a new program feature is added, a new module or hierarchy of modules to perform that feature is added.
3. Program testing and retesting is easier.
4. Program errors are easier to locate and correct.
5. Program efficiency is easier to improve.

Control Functions

It might seem inconceivable that any program can be broken down into three general patterns or functions, but that is the case (Bohm and Jacopini 1966). A module can perform one or more actions in sequence, or it can do a repeated series of actions using a loop, or it can control a branch depending on conditions. Each of these functions needs special attention.

Action. An action module is one that consists of one or activities such as PRINT, LET, READ, etc., which are always done in the same sequence. Using a structured flowchart, an action module might be seen as:

Calculate A = B + C
Print A

This diagram says that the first module has one entry point, and once entered, a value is calculated for A. In the second module, the value is printed out, and the module is exited. Each rectangle represents an action block, and the overall rectangle is a logical action block as well, even though it represents a sequence of actions. A series of action blocks may be subsumed into a single block for clarity of flow; but if this is done, it should be clear that a series of functions is being performed. Action blocks can be placed within other blocks or modules as is appropriate. Keep in mind that an action block is entered from the top and exited at the bottom.

Loop. A second type of control function is the loop used to perform a repetitious sequence. Generically, a loop is characterized by (1) an initialization set; (2) a condition requirement; (3) the scope of the repetition; (4) an increment step. The actual command and sequence of events is a characteristic of the high-order programming language being used. Some common looping commands are FOR/NEXT, REPEAT/UNTIL, DO/WHILE, PERFORM/UNTIL, etc. In BASIC, the most common, and sometimes the only available structure is the FOR/NEXT command.

The structured flowchart for a generic FOR/NEXT loop is:

Initialize System
Set Termination Condition
Specify Scope of the Iteration
Increment
Condition Check

In this diagram, the outside rectangle represents the module. The inside rectangles represent the functions performed in the iteration. The space to the left of the inside rectangles indicates that everything to the right is done as long as the termination condition for the block does not hold true. If the example for a FOR/NEXT iteration that was used in Chapter 2:

```
100   FOR X = 1 TO 3
110   LET A = A + X
120   LET B = A + X
130   NEXT X
```

were to be shown as a structured flowchart, it would be:

LET X = 1	Step 1
FOR X ≤ 3	Step 2
LET A = A + X	Step 3
LET B = A + X	Step 4
LET X = X + 1 (Increment)	Step 5
Is X > 3 (Condition Check)	Step 6

This diagram indicates that at Step 1, the system is initialized by setting X equal to 1. Step 2 sets the termination condition for the loop, i.e., X greater than 3. Steps 3 and 4 are the scope of the loop, each step being its own action module and represented by a single small rectangle. Each action module is performed in sequence. The next rectangle in the sequence is different because it is unique in incrementing the loop counter; finally, the check is made to see if the condition for the loop still holds.

Visually, this is an excellent representation of the iteration. To begin with, the initialization of the loop, Step 1, is clearly outside the main body of the loop, and it is executed only once in the overall module. The scope of the loop is also clearly viewed as a separate sequence of operations all embedded within the same module. There is one possible area of confusion: whether the termination condition for the loop is checked before entry into the scope sequence, or as part of the scope sequence. In some iterations, the conditions of the loop are checked before any of the action modules are executed. With a FOR/NEXT loop, the termination condition is not checked until the scope is completed, and this scope sequence includes the incrementing of the counter. It should be obvious from the diagram that iterations could be done in other ways.

If all loops followed this pattern, the problem would be minor, but unfortunately the sequence varies according to the command structure that is used for the iteration. For the following module:

$$
\begin{array}{ll}
90 & \text{LET X} = 1 \\
100 & \text{WHILE X} \leqslant 3 \text{ DO} \\
110 & \text{LET A} = \text{A} + \text{X} \\
120 & \text{LET B} = \text{A} + \text{X} \\
130 & \text{THEN}
\end{array}
$$

The structured flowchart would be:

LET X = 1
WHILE X ≤ 3 DO
Is X > 3 (Condition Check)
LET A = A + X
LET B = A + X
LET X = X + 1 (Increment)

This example does not look very different from the previous diagram for the FOR/NEXT loop, but there is one significant change: the sequence of events is different. The termination condition of the loop is checked prior to entering the scope of the loop. In practice, the loop can be skipped without being executed because the terminating condition is checked prior to the first execution of the scope. This is never the case with the FOR/NEXT loop: it is executed at least once before the termination condition is checked.

Branch. A third control structure is the branch. This is the structure that truly differentiates a computer from a calculator. The computer can be programmed to make decisions based on conditions. In BASIC, the common decision command is IF/THEN. The decision is always based upon an examination of the argument of the IF command. The choices are either/or. The condition is true and one thing happens or the condition is false and something else happens. The conditions may be complex, but the decision process is straightforward.

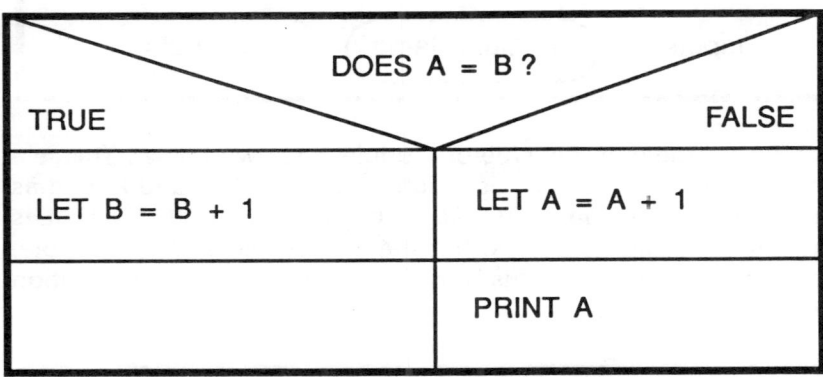

The large rectangle represents the module. The triangle in the top center is the initial step in the module where the condition is checked. If the condition is true, the set of modules to the left are executed in the sequence shown; if the condition is false, the modules to the right are executed in the sequence shown. The number of modules in either set is of no consequence; one set can be null. What is important is that the execution of the module result in one or the other sequence being executed, not both.

The CASE command which is available in some languages is a more elaborate form of the branch structure where there are more than two choices in the module; the module is then a series of mutually exclusive branches. The computer moves through the CASE structure by making a series of branch decisions. The CASE representation is a convenience for the programmer when it is available, but it is not fundamentally different from the branch control structure.

Invocation

In addition to modules and control functions, structured programs have other underlying concepts, the most significant being invocation. Invocation is that concept which describes or determines the relationships between modules. The assumption of an invocation is that when a module is called from an action module, the control of the computer is passed on to the called module until its function is completed, then control is returned to the original module of the sequence. Diagrammatically this would be:

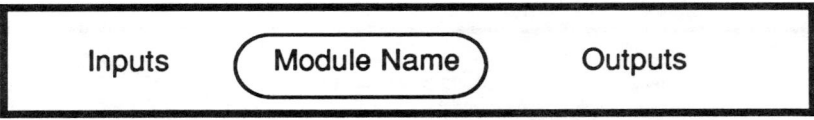

An example of this type of module is shown below. This is a simple module which has as inputs values for A, B and X, and as output a variable named TOTAL. It may be thought that TOTAL is the sum of A and B and X, but that is not necessarily so. Total could be the sum of A^2 plus B^2 plus X^2 or almost any combination of the three variables.

The actual function of the module SUM is not important at this level of abstraction. In fact, one of the purposes of the diagrams is that they make it easier to see the flow of the program without getting involved in the details; this perspective allows the programmer to see the overall design.

Argument Passing. Invocation also involves passing information from one module to another. For example, a programmer might be using the variable **N** to represent the number of grades in a gradebook program, and he adds a new module to the program which deals with the same number of grades, but the new module is written using **NG** for the number of grades. The variables **N** and **NG** could be local variables if their values are limited to a particular module. Putting aside recoding the module, it is possible with some languages to pass the value of **N** to **NG** without changing any of the code in the new module.

When the system can handle the "passing," it is typically done by organizing the sequence of variables in the first module so that those in the second module are in the same sequence. The sequence determines the assignment of values, not the names of the variables. The fact that typical dialects of BASIC do not provide for argument passing is a serious limitation of the language for the development of subroutine libraries and large programs involving multiple modules.

(A word of caution to those who might not be familiar with argument passing; if a value is passed to a module and the value is changed in some way within the module, that does not necessarily mean that the new value for the variable will be returned to the original variable in the calling module.)

Recursion. Another case of invocation occurs when a module can call upon itself as part of a sequence of action modules; this feature is called recursion. Recursion allows for the writing of very concise code when dealing with factoring or repeated calculations. Mathematicians get very excited about recursion, but there is very little, if anything, that recursion can do that cannot be done by a computer through simple iteration.

An example of the application of recursion is a module that yields N factorial or N! {N! = n × (n − 1) × (n − 2) ... 3 × 2 × 1}. Remember, the typical computer at the machine level does not multiply more than two number at a time. In order to calculate N! on the computer, one would go through a sequence of first multiplying n by (n − 1), then taking the result and multiplying it by (n − 2), then taking that result and multiplying by (n − 3), etc., until the value of the multiplicand becomes 1. The gist of the problem certainly suggests iteration; the orderly sequence might suggest that a routine could be developed that recurs in a regular fashion starting with n = N and continuing to n = 1.

The structured flowchart for a factorial module is shown below:

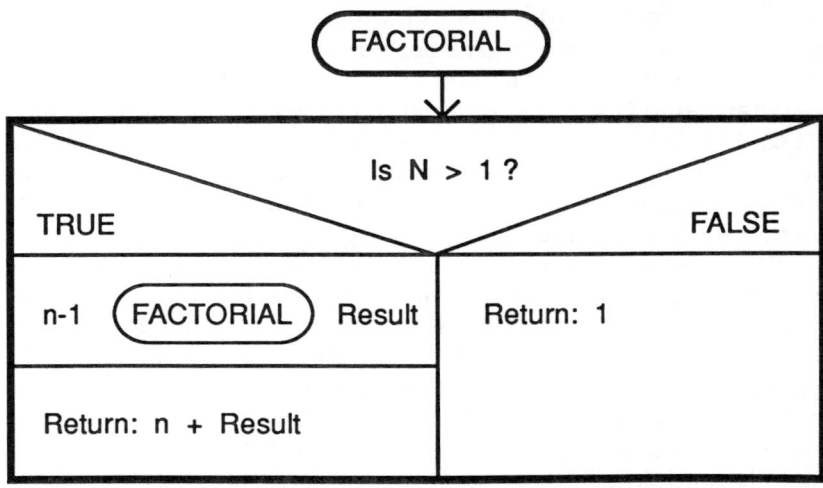

The significant element in this diagram is that the module FACTORIAL is called from within the module. The same result might be achieved using iteration with the factorial module shown below:

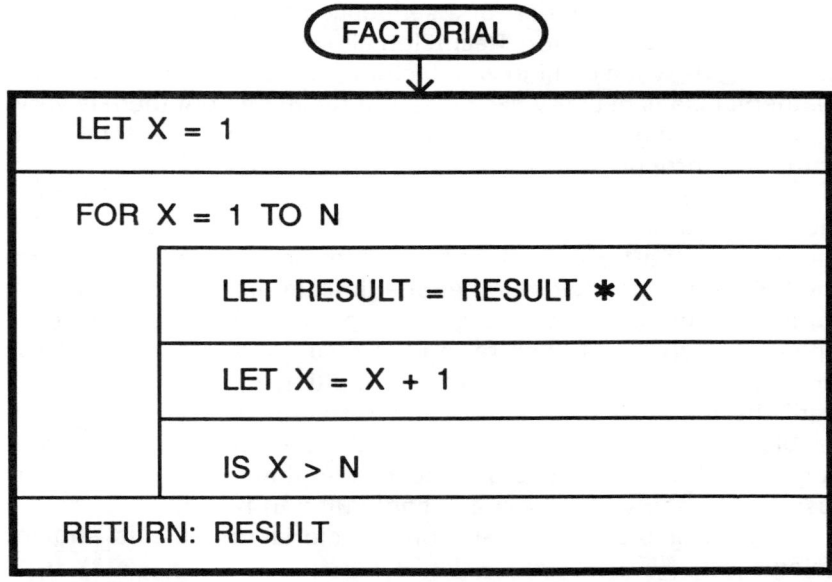

Although the results would be identical, the actual process within the computer handling these two modules is very different. In the case of the iteration, the process involves a simple loop which builds upon itself. In the recursion approach, the process would involve a series of independent operations which would be accomplished by repeated calls to the same module, which in fact is the module from which the call originates, until terminal condition (n = 1) is met.

Recursion is such a significant aspect of structured programming that it needs some special elaboration. There are two different formats for recursion—embedded and tail.

Let us assume we are interested in the value of 5! and we are using the above module. In the first call of the module, the value of n is known to be 5, but the value of (n − 1)! is not known and the process requires that 5 be multiplied by (n − 1)!. With recursion, the computer stores all the necessary information for keeping track of the present condition, namely n = 5, until a value can be obtained for (n − 1)!. The computer then goes to the called routine and executes it for (n − 1). The sequence is repeated, the computer determines the value for n, which at this point is 4, but in order to do this it requires the value of (n − 1)! or 3!. Again the information is temporarily stored until a value of (n − 1)! can be obtained. In terms of internal processing, it is important that the second iteration of the subroutine does not interfere with the first.

The computer at this stage needs to store partial data for both sets of conditions, i.e., for n = 5 and n = 4 while it proceeds to determine a value for n = 3. The sequence is repeated as required until the terminal condition of the recursion is met, in the case in point when n = 1 and the value of n! is known, that is n! = 1.

In our example, the process proceeded "down" the recursion until N! = 1. At this point, the process was reversed and the value for the step 2 · (n − 1)! was determined (2 · 1). The product here is then used for the next step up in the recursion, and so on.

What can be imagined here is that the sequence is a series of steps to lower and lower levels, each step getting closer to the terminal condition for the sequence. The value of the function at each step is unknown because it is dependent on the value of the next lowest step. Once the terminal condition is met, the value of the lowest step is known. The subsequent values for each of the intermediate steps can then be calculated, and the series of cal-culations are made until the value required to satisfy the initial call of the subroutine is returned to the calling module.

The concept of recursion is both powerful and elegant. It is powerful in that a recursive routine call be used to calculate very complex and exhausting numerical problems with minimum pro-gramming. Recursion is elegant in that the actual coding of the routines is so simple and direct that it communicates to the reader the process in a clear and concise manner. This is very important in programming, but a caveat about using recursion is in order.

First, in terms of the power of the programming, the coding can be very simple, but it belies the complexity of the processing and the demands that it places on the system. A recursion that requires a program to go to a depth of 100 levels, i.e., N! when N = 100, requires that the computer retain the information for each level. It is analogous to going down a flight a stairs; each step would hold partial information necessary when the steps are re-traced before leaving the module after reaching the limits of the recursion. The storage of this partial information can tax the avail-able memory of a microcomputer. (Some operating systems use a fixed length stack for recursion that can be very restrictive.) A less elegant loop might be used to accomplish the same ends without encumbering as much memory.

The second limitation imposed by recursion is that the coding might only be intelligible to those readers understanding recursion as a mathematical construct or process. The proponents of the language LOGO are quick to point out the availability of recursion, and its integral role in the application of the language. They sug-gest, based on the ability of young students to use recursion in solving problems, that the concept can be learned through an exploratory approach as recommended by Papert (1980). The abili-ty of students to use recursion to draw complex and attractive patterns and designs is one thing; the ability of students to un-derstand recursion as an elegant mathematic construct and a use-ful programming concept is another. Kurland and Pea (1985) have shown that students had a misguided "looping" interpretation of LOGO recursion, and that their mental model persisted even after contradictory evidence was presented.

There is little evidence that the concept of recursion can be learned by elementary school children, and certainly there is no evidence that a student can learn the concept using a free, ex-ploratory mode of instruction. True, students can use recursion on a trial and error basis, but the available experimental evidence does not show that they understand what is happening.

It should be pointed out that there are two distinct ways that recursion is used in programs. In the factorial example in this chapter, the recursion calls were done within the process of the execution of the recursion. The recursion in this situation is said to be embedded; the processing is delayed until the conditions specified in the module are met. For example, the multiplication of n by (n − 1)! is delayed until a value is determined for (n − 1)!, which is delayed until (n − 2)! has been calculated. Each call of the recursion is delayed until the condition is met, then the calculations are done in reverse order. The analogy of going down a flight of steps and then retracing them applies to embedded recursion. If the recursion calls for a series of calculations, typically the lowest step in the recursion is actually calculated first.

The other form of recursion occurs when the call is done after an action or calculation has been completed, so that the progression through the recursive module is a sequence of activity which continues until the specified condition is met. In this case, drawing on the step analogy, as each step is encountered going down, some action is initiated before the recursive call. This is known as tail recursion.

The following two procedures borrowed from a study by Kurland and Pea (1985) illustrate the difference between the two forms of recursion. You may want to determine the output from each before they are discussed. The first listing is an example of a tail recursion procedure where :SIDE = 80.

```
TO SHAPEB   :SIDE
    IF SIDE = 20 STOP
    REPEAT 4 [FORWARD :SIDE RIGHT 90]
    RIGHT 90 FORWARD :SIDE LEFT 90
    SHAPEB :SIDE/2
END
```

The next listing is an example of an embedded recursion procedure where :SIDE = 80.

```
TO SHAPEC   :SIDE
    IF SIDE = 20 STOP
    SHAPE C   :SIDE/2
```

REPEAT 4 [FORWARD :SIDE RIGHT 90]
RIGHT 90 FORWARD   :SIDE LEFT 90
       END

These examples clearly demonstrate the recursion concept. In the first case, the tail recursion, the program draws a square with a side equal to 80, then on the second call it draws another square of side 40, and on the third call it stops. The module is executed as it is called. Although the outcome is what we might expect in a simple loop, the program is not.

This is not the case with the embedded recursion. The first call sets the side equal to 80, but before drawing a square, a second call is made with side equal to 40, then a third call with side equal to 20. At this point, the calls are executed beginning with the last with side equal to 40, and then a box with side equal 80. Although this outcome could be produced by a loop, the loop would not be straightforward because the process is not a simple iteration.

Nesting. The use of rectangles as the characteristic shape of modules in structured flowcharting makes it possible to build complex modules out of simple modules and create larger pieces of a program without resorting to formatting changes. The nesting of modules, each with its own function, permits easier visualization of a program, avoiding the complications of the syntax and coding.

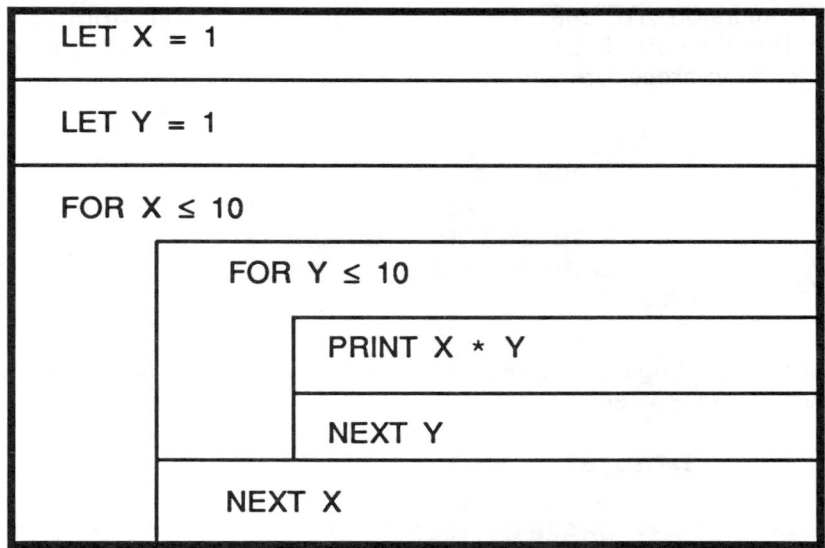

Top-Down Design

The final structured programming concept involves the planning of the overall design of a program. The overriding concept is that a program should be designed from the most general to the most specific activity. Just as the programmer should first decide about the function of a module before becoming involved in the code and syntax, the planning of the modules themselves should be done only after the general flow of the program has been prepared.

A program should be planned from its most abstract parts first and the most specific and detailed aspects last. The first step is to prepare a hierarchical chart showing the relationship among the various segments of the program and the relationships of the modules. The goal is to reduce a large complex programming problem into a set of simpler short programming segments. This approach is commonly known as top-down design; it requires the generic problem-solving skill of analysis.

The first stage of a top-down approach to design is a chart made up of a series of blocks which typically show the development of the program from the top of the page to the bottom. The upper blocks represent general ideas, or possibly program menus; the lowermost blocks represent actual modules that would exist in the program. The lines connecting the blocks show the operational flow of the program.

The hierarchical nature of top-down design is shown in a series of rules which govern the relationships between modules.

Rule 1: At the top of the structured chart is a single module which contains the main program and the branches to the logical program functions.

This top module is said to be at Level 0. (Some formulations call this Level 1, and subsequent levels are all increased accordingly.) It is always executed when the program is run. It is the most general of all the modules, and it frequently controls the flow of the entire program.

Rule 2: At a level immediately below the main program is a
series of modules which correspond to the major functions that are performed by the program.

The second level modules are given a status of Level 1. They
are always called from the main program module, and control is
always transferred back to the main module, never between Level
1 modules, even if the sequence in the program might be from
one Level 1 module to another Level 1 module. The main program
module always controls execution of Level 1 modules.

Rule 3: At the next highest level are those modules that are
needed to execute the functions of Level 1 operations.

Level 2 modules can only be executed when there is an explicit
call from a Level 1 module; they are never invoked by a Level 0
call. In some situations a Level 2 module might be called from
more than one Level 1 module, but the transfer of control within
the program must be such that it returns to the module from which
it was called.

Rule 4: There can be no loops built into the control structure
of the program.

Modules that are part of the control structure of the program
cannot call themselves nor can they call any module that has called
them at some higher level of the control structure. This should not
be interpreted as a rule prohibiting recursion. Recursion is a powerful technique, but its function is to perform a single activity, albeit
repeatedly, and therefore needs to be subsumed within a module.
Recursion is a function that either returns a value or performs an
operation; it is not a control function. Recursion does not have a
role in terms of program flow, and therefore it does not have a
role in the hierarchy chart used for organizing top-down programs.
Recursion might best be viewed as a complex mathematical function which has inputs and outputs just as any other function.

At this point it is appropriate to point out that a module is not
a synonym for a subroutine. True, many modules are subroutines,
but only when the module performs a specific function that can
be reduced to a limited number of lines of code. Subroutines might
best be thought of as being between a module and a built-in system
algorithm. A complex subroutine could be a module, and could be

represented in a top-down diagram as a separate block. On the other hand, when a subroutine is used to perform a single operation, such as summing up a column in a table, which yields a single value or outcome, it is not limited to an operational function in the program.

It should be noted that some experts suggest that there are times when the bottom-up approach can be used effectively, particularly when a problem has many elements in common with known problems and solutions. Considering the limited experience of novices, and the tendency of self-taught programmers to avoid planning, introductory courses will probably continue to emphasize top-down design.

In addition to using a top-down approach, the design process includes consideration of alternative solutions and a means of selecting the best design. The latter activity is in part based on an understanding of the particulars of a variety of programming languages and some insight into the processing that would be required of the computer.

For novice programmers, the language requirements typically relate to the built-in function, primitives, that are available in the language being studied; and their knowledge of algorithms appropriate to the problem. More advanced students might be asked to include in their design of a program a rationale for the selection of a programming language.

Understanding computer operations requires that a programmer develop a "mental model" of the internal operations. The use of a mental model is a long-standing intellectual tool for dealing with abstract concepts. Models and analogies as instructional devices will be discussed in the next chapter on classroom learning.

At this point it is sufficient to say that although the top-down approach is the key component of programming design, program design requires a set of skills making it a more demanding task than might first be apparent. Dalbey and Linn (1985, 257), as a result of their review of the research on program design, suggest that the skills and conceptualizations required are not typically practiced in other problem-solving domains.

Well-Structured Programs

All things considered, what are the characteristics of a well-structured program? Is there a checklist that would allow us to evaluate a program to determine whether it meets some standard or set of guidelines? Obviously, the answer must be yes or the issue would not have been raised. Borrowing again from Martin and McClure (1983, 81), here are the six properties of a well-structured program.

- The program is divided into a set of modules arranged in a hierarchy that defines the logical relationships and the flow of the executed program.
- The executed flow from module to module is restricted to a simple, easily understood scheme in which control must enter the module at a single entry point, must leave the module from a single exit point, and control must always be passed back to the invoking module.
- Module construction is standardized according to the traditional modularization rules and legal program constructs are restricted to action, repetition, and branching. Modules may contain more than one control function.
- Each program variable serves only one program purpose and the scope of a variable (i.e. the set of modules in which the variable is assessed) is apparent and limited.
- Documentation is required in the source code to introduce each module by explaining its function, its data requirements (inputs and outputs), and its invocation relationship to other modules in the program.

In an introductory course at the high school level, it remains unclear how much depth can be achieved in following structured programming principles and processes, but they surely should not be neglected or ignored when they can just as easily be incorporated into the curriculum. As is the case with most of the concepts developed for structured programming, the ideas themselves are simple enough that they often do not require an explanation or commentary. If it were not for this simplicity, they could not be recommended as part of the curriculum for beginning programmers.

WRITING CODE

There is a tendency, particularly when working in a language like BASIC, to go from a general idea of what a program might be like to writing the instructions or code. If Microsoft BASIC has left a legacy, it is that self-taught programmers want to enter code, not to plan; nothing counts but what can be seen on the monitor, the rest is just superfluous theory. For the "hacker", programming is a trial-and-error operation validated by a program that is apparently error-free and produces the desired result—nothing else really matters.

These attitudes and processes may work when the program is less than fifty lines; possibly an especially good hacker can manage a program of up to a hundred lines of unstructured, unplanned code, but at some point the size leads to unmanageable programs. Syntactical and logical errors lead to uncontrollable or embedded bugs and unpredictable losses of time and energy in trying to correct them. Even when the program does run, if the overall structure is lacking, modification and maintenance may consume as much time and energy as the initial programming.

Beginning students should be taught to develop programs using the techniques that have been found to produce efficient results by professional programmers. In addition to structuring techniques which add to clarity and understanding, students recognize the need to include commentary, explanations and guides for those who read their program. The methods of documentation presented here are those that have proven successful with beginning students and in retraining students who learned programming using a trial-and-error approach.

Input/Process/Output Forms

Early concerns with spaghetti code led to the teaching of flowcharting. Some teachers still use flowcharting as a means of showing the logical order within a program. Flowcharting provides a student with an idea of the step-by-step logic of a program and may be a good learning or debugging technique, but as most programmers know, flowcharting does not give an overview of the program nor the relationships that exist between the parts. Shneiderman et al. (1977) have shown that flowcharting does not make a difference in college students' ability to learn programming.

Frequently flowcharting has been employed to document a program or as a technique for uncovering logical errors. More often than not, flowcharting was done after the program was written and tried; usually only when the errors could not be fixed by other means.

One of the structured programmer's alternatives to flowchart-

HIPO DIAGRAM

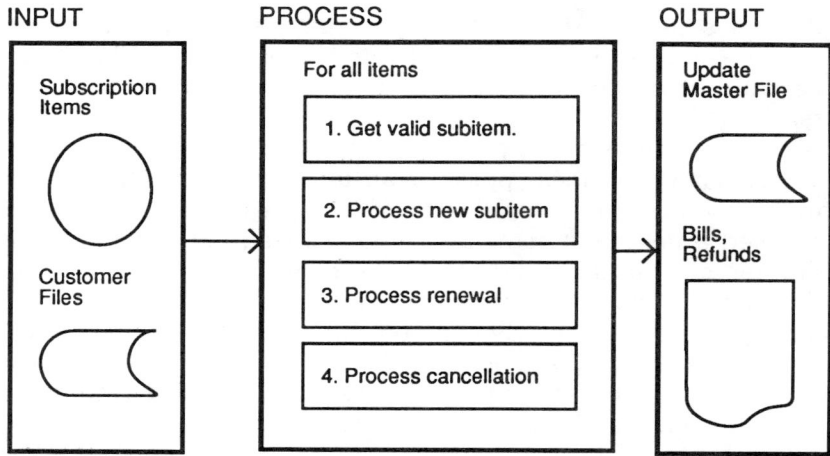

Figure 3.7. *Hierarchy plus Input-Process-Output (HIPO) Diagram*

ing is the input/process/output form or IPO. Each module in a program is viewed as a separate program with its own internal structure. This structure has at least three components; input, process, and output. In designing a module, the programmer is asked to describe each of the three components using a prescribed form. Although the form itself is not standardized, the general idea is consistent.

In some cases, the form is horizontal, and the flow within the form proceeds from left to right. Martin and McClure (1983) recommend such a chart as part of their documentation package for a program. In their particular configuration, shown in Figure 3.7, the diagram utilizes flowcharting symbols to further visualize the workings of the module.

It might be assumed that the module presented in Figure 3.7 would be a level 2 or below in the top-down structure, and that some of the elements in the module would be either subroutines or modules further down in the hierarchy. In a comprehensive system, the elements of the module would be coded according to the level and schema in the overall design of the program.

An alternative form that has been used with high school students is shown in Figure 3.8. Beginning students can be taught to use this form for even the simplest of programs. A teacher might

```
| Program: _____   Date: _____ |
| Module: _____   Author: ____  |
|------------------------------------|
| Function                           |
|------------------------------------|
| Input:                             |
|------------------------------------|
| Process                            |
|                                    |
|                                    |
|                                    |
|------------------------------------|
| Output                             |
|                                    |
|                                    |
|------------------------------------|
| Approval: _____ Date: ____  |
```

Figure 3.8. *IPO Form for individual modules.*

not only require that an IPO (Input/Process/Output) form like that shown in Figure 3.8 be submitted for each module that is entered into the computer, but also ask each student, or groups of students if they are working in teams, to have their plans reviewed and approved by another student(s) before the code is entered.

The purpose of the IPO forms is to provide details on the logic of the individual module, but their greatest value may be in the specification of the inputs and outputs, because it is these details that enable the modules to be integrated into larger programs. A good activity which can make this clear to students is to develop a program for a simple game. After the necessary modules are agreed upon, have the class break up into teams to design them. Once the modules are put together to form the final program, it will quickly become apparent that, although each module might work independently, unless there has been planning and coordination among groups, the composite will be a disaster.

In the classroom, the IPO can be used in conjunction with pseudocode and walkthroughs, as will be described below, to produce an ongoing process that is not labor intensive for the instructor. At the same time it can produce a procedure for review, feedback, and formative evaluation.

Pseudocode

The second phase of writing code is the preparation of pseudocode. Pseudocode is a narrative form of programming in which the programmer describes the steps in the process using language which is more descriptive of the process than reflective of a particular language.

Using an IPO form, the process is described in a series of simple sentences or phrases which eventually will be translated to actual lines of code. Where applicable, indentation and internal documentation are included on the form. The pseudocode tells the reader the detailed steps that will take place in the module.

Protocols for pseudocode are not fixed, but Campell (1984, 137) suggests that certain key words be used to provide consistent expressions for loops and decision points, and that these key words might be highlighted with upper case letters. Just as in the case of the final code, it is preferred that the unconditional jump be avoided, especially if the referenced location is in another module.

Figure 3.9 presents an example of pseudocode prepared for a module that generates a random number between 1 and 6 for two dice to be used in a game simulation.

SUBROUTINE: DICE VALUE

DIE 1
LET a number **D1** be selected at random
      convert it into an integer
      check to see **IF** it is less than 1
            IF less than 1 **GOTO DIE** 1
      check to see **IF** it is greater than 6
            IF greater than 6 **GOTO DIE** 1
DIE 2
LET a second number **D2** be selected at random
      convert it into an integer
      check to see **IF** it is less than 1
            IF less than 1 **GOTO DIE** 2
      check to see **IF** it is greater than 6
            IF greater than 6 **GOTO DIE** 2
RETURN to calling module

Figure 3.9. Pseudocode for a Number Generating Module

Once the pseudocode has been reviewed, possibly by means of a walkthrough as will be discussed below, it will be translated into a form that can be understood by the computer. For example, it might be translated into BASIC as shown in Figure 3.10. In this case, the higher order language was anticipated by the use and highlighting of key words in the pseudocode.

```
REM SUBROUTINE DICE VALUE
LET D1 = RND (A)
LET D1 = INT (D1)
IF D1 < 1 THEN GOTO line ...
IF D1 > 6 THEN GOTO line ...
LET D2 = RND (A)
LET D2 = INT (D2)
IF D2 < 1 THEN GOTO line ...
IF D2 > 6 THEN GOTO line ...
RETURN
```

Figure 3.10. BASIC Code for a Number Generating Module

In a way, pseudocode is a form of outlining which allows the student to organize his thoughts without becoming overwhelmed with the form and syntax of the final program. It provides an intermediate step in the solution of a problem, resulting in a product that can be analyzed and modified if necessary before committing to a final solution. The use of intermediate goals and structured processes are problem-solving techniques worthy of note.

Walkthroughs

Every programmer has had the experience of being unable to resolve a problem with a program; but as soon as he started to explain the situation to a colleague, the error became apparent. Or else, the problem was quickly solved by a listener who reduced the difficulty to a trivial oversight through some insight that had eluded the programmer. Having colleagues involved in program development certainly has merit; many developers have incorporated peer input as a regular part of program development instead of waiting until a program is in need of repair.

Using a process similar to brainstorming, software developers have devised a technique known as the walkthrough, in which a programmer has a group of peers review his pseudocode (IPO forms) while he articulates the flow of the program. The walkthrough participants are encouraged to raise questions and make suggestions, but not to become involved in details of syntax or coding. The programmer assumes a position of explaining what he is doing, but at the same time remains open to suggestions and criticisms. All comments and suggestions are noted for consideration, to be dealt with at a future time.

Depending on the complexity of the program being reviewed, the walkthrough process will be more or less structured according to locally accepted practice. It is common to have a review form, to have someone keep records of the input, and to have a fixed time limit for the meeting. It is suggested that 30 minutes be a maximum allotted time. The idea of the walkthrough is to eliminate as many logical errors as possible before a module is committed to code.

Karl Jahns (1985) has incorporated the use of IPOs and walkthroughs as part of his programming classes for junior and senior high school students. The students are organized into teams, and the teams meet on a regular basis during their laboratory time to review each others IPOs. Students do not enter their programs into the computer until the pseudocode has been reviewed and approved by other members of their team. He claims that the practice has increased the efficiency of his students because many errors in logic are removed before the coding is done. The same benefits are claimed by professional programmers who use structuring techniques.

It is interesting to note that the level of programming reported in Karl Jahns' classes is significantly higher than most. One of the assignments is to write pseudocode for a program that will find and display the circumference and the area of a circle, given the radius. This is followed by a program that simulates a bank machine, which asks for a code number, matches it to a list of users, checks the balance in the account, and permits a withdrawal if sufficient funds are available.

In this approach, the problems of syntax and typing are deferred while the student is learning the higher order techniques of pseudocoding and structured walkthrough. These are problem-solving skills with the potential not only for transfer across languages, but possibly across subjects and disciplines.

Weiland (1983) suggests the following rules and guidelines for walkthroughs:

1. Meetings are brief to keep energy levels high.
2. Meetings are frequent so that work gets reviewed promptly.
3. Materials for review are distributed a day or so in advance.
4. No managers with hiring/firing authority are included. (In an academic setting, no one with grading authority is included.) Participants come from a peer group, which minimizes pressure.
5. Attention is exclusively directed to finding bugs, not to fixing them nor to discussing matters of taste or style. One useful device is to limit discussion of any topic to three minutes or less. "Works" vs. "Doesn't Work" can generally be decided in this amount of time.
6. Criticisms are directed to the product, not the producer. Questions begin "I don't understand . . . " not "Why did you . . . "
7. Any bugs found are written down in the meeting notes, called a Walkthrough Conference Report Form, for use by the product's author (see Figure 3.11). All participants sign the notes, saying in effect, "I have inspected this product and, except for the points noted, I accept it and take joint responsibility for its quality."

This process can easily be modified for a classroom setting. In fact, the walkthrough process can be an excellent classroom management tool because the students monitor each others' progress, and provide the formative evaluation that is virtually impossible for a teacher with thirty students. It is recommended that when groups are used, they be reconstituted at least once a quarter, and possibly with each assignment, so that students do not get caught up in personality conflicts which would be uncomfortable for prolonged periods.

Group activities are especially useful when computer access is limited. "Off-line" organization and planning needs to be focused; the walkthrough can provide focus and at the same time involve the students in an activity which models the real world of programmers.

Another advantage of the walkthrough is that it tends to offset the caricature of programmers as being introverts who work in

---

Teaching Computer Science   **Structured Programming**

STRUCTURED WALKTHROUGH REPORT

Project: _____Product:_____

Date: _____/_____/_____   Time: ____:_____

	Signature	Name

Presenter: _____ _____

Moderator:_____ _____

Recorder: _____ _____

Participant: _____ _____

Participant: _____ _____

Participant: _____ _____

ACTION POINTS:

1. _____

2. _____

3. _____

4. _____

5. _____

6. _____

7. _____

8. _____

DISPOSITION: _____ Accepted   _____ Accepted with Revisions Above

_____ Major Revisions and Further Walkthrough Needed

OTHER REMARKS: _____

_____

_____

_____

_____

Figure 3.11. *Walkthrough Conference Report Form*

isolation. Shneiderman (1980) suggested that although this may have been the case with some of the programming pioneers, the need to meet production schedules and to provide errorless code has led to wider utilization of team processes. It is important not only to teach students to program, but to give them a realistic view of the workplace. Modeling software engineering techniques in the classroom addresses this objective as well.

Syntax

Strangely enough, the learning of syntax and the actual writing of the code becomes a minor part of a course in which structured programming and problem solving are the goals. In some colleges, the introductory courses in programming are given without any actual programs being written, and in other colleges, the choice of programming language is left to the individual student with no formal instruction provided in syntax. These are extreme strategies, possibly due to lack of sufficient hardware to provide access for novices. In any case, these extremes are not strategies that have been demonstrated to be effective at the high school level or below.

Students take programming courses because they want to write programs that work. They are anxious to be at the keyboard, and they want to be successful. The latter is the motivation for imposing the structured approach on students. Not only should the program run, but the program should be organized and planned so that it runs the first time. To run successfully the first time it is tried, a program must be well planned and the student must use the right syntax.

The learning of syntax cannot be overlooked, but it helps to consider it the means to an end, not the end itself. A course that is graded strictly on tests involving syntax, and on whether a programming assignment runs will not develop problem-solving skills, and it will not give an honest view of what it means to program. With these caveats in mind, the formal teaching of syntax can be dealt with on a need-to-know basis. Teach those commands necessary to solve a particular problem, and provide access to the entire range of commands.

When the opportunity presents itself, provide the students with the most user-friendly editor available. In time, it will be possible to teach programming with languages that are closer to natural language than BASIC; in the meantime, students may have to be satisfied with a minimum editor like the one available with Microsoft BASIC.

If the available editor does not help with syntax, then help sheets or posters can be used so that when a syntax error occurs, the student can efficiently find the information he needs. To downplay the importance of syntax, students might be given summary sheets of all commands; these can be used both at the terminals and during tests. Some teachers may prefer to have their students prepare their own summary sheets, which they are free to use at anytime.

In the previous chapter, general ideas on teaching syntax were developed. It is unnecessary to repeat the specifics, but it should be noted that there is a difference in the sequence in which commands are taught—this is determined by the kinds of assignments, and the students' need for certain commands—and the storage and recall of this same information, which is dictated more by the functions they perform.

It is helpful to students to organize commands, with their syntax and limitations, according to function, as was done in Chapter 2.

Debugging

It is not of the nature of a computer program to have bugs, despite the seemingly overwhelming evidence to the contrary. Bugs occur in programs only if they are put there by the programmer. The process described for developing a structured program is a major attempt to prepare programs that are as error-free as possible. The goal, as stated earlier, is to write code that will run on the first try, and meet the specifications.

Studies of debugging have shown that novices and experts tend to make the same number of errors, the difference is in their ability to discover the errors. A characteristic of expert programmers is the ability to identify and remove bugs quickly. Dalbey and Linn (1985, 260) have identified the following skills associated with the debugging process: using feedback effectively, identifying patterns and inconsistencies, using deduction and inference, challenging assumptions, and seeking improbable alternatives. Obviously these are skills worth teaching.

Syntax Errors. The most trivial, but nevertheless common, error is that involving the actual writing of code. It can be anything from a typo to the failure to insert a comma or a semicolon where required.

One of the differences between a microcomputer editor and one that is available on minicomputers is the ability of the more sophisticated computer to detect error in syntax at the time a line of code is entered. On most microcomputers, the error is not found until the program is actually run.

Teachers should fight the tendency <u>not</u> to inform students of their typos and syntactical errors, and should point them out directly or at least pose a question that indicates the solution. <u>Asking students to "discover" rules and protocols of syntax is not an efficient way to teach</u>, nor is it consistent with the goals of a programming course in which one objective is to teach problem-solving skills. Some teachers seem to think that the problem-solving skills that are claimed for computer science are learned through solving the problems associated with using proper syntax. Syntax bugs are information or reference problems, not conceptual or logic errors, and they will not be resolved efficiently through trial and error. It would be ridiculous to ask a student who was the sixteenth president of the United States, and if he didn't know, expect him to guess names until, through trial and error, he came up with the correct answer. Why do teachers expect students to guess the correct syntax for a programming command?

Learning syntax is like learning the alphabet; of itself it has little or no value. Children like to say the alphabet when they first learn it, but if it were not for the fact that they learned the letter sequence, it would be a meaningless accomplishment. Learning the syntax of BASIC, or any other language, is only slightly more useful at best.

Interface. The second level of errors involves the interfacing between the various modules in a program. It is absolutely essential that the calls from the various modules to their subordinate modules, from level 1 to level 2 or level 2 to level 3, be executed as designed. This can be checked without waiting for an entire program to be written.

The process is called top-down testing, and it is accomplished by preparing a series of "dummy" modules, sometimes called <u>studs</u>, which occupy the lower level modules and are called while an upper level module is being tested.

In debugging, or for that matter in the development stage, the lower level modules can be tested and a trace message, a constant value, or a limited response that might be typical of its desired product can be returned. A good example of this can be found in Appendix C where, in the Structured Basic Development System, the student prepares dummy modules that print trace messages before the development of the actual modules themselves is undertaken.

TESTING

After the actual code is written, and the program is run without terminating abruptly, the final stage in the development cycle is to test the program to see if the results are as expected. In a sense, this is a debugging process, but the objective here is to determine the ability of the program to perform as specified, not simply to run without crashing.

The first test should be a "good data" test in which a set of data of known validity is entered, and the results checked against known results. This process is repeated as often as necessary to test the extreme or boundary conditions that have been specified for the program. Sample input and output should be recorded and stored as part of the external documentation for the program.

If unexpected results occur at this point, the system can be examined in the same way as suggested in the previous section under debugging, using traces, constants for variables and/or simplification of functions. The objective here is to identify the module that is malfunctioning. One of the advantages of structured programming is that the independence built into the individual modules makes it easier to isolate the sources of error.

A common error-detecting technique is to test a module as if it were an independent program. The module is isolated from the main program—the unconditional jump is very useful at this stage—and dummy values are supplied for each of the variables as needed. Again, through the use of the IPO forms and internal documentation to be discussed below, the process described allows quick identification of input requirements for each module.

Once the program has been demonstrated to respond to good data as might be expected, the program should be checked for its performance when inappropriate data is used. Inappropriate data may be values that extend beyond the specified range, partially correct or inconsistent data, or data that might result from poor data-entry techniques.

DOCUMENTATION

Development of any software program or package should include proper documentation. According to Martin and McClure (1983, 174), the purpose of documentation is "to make programs more readable by people so that they can be understood, corrected, modified, tested and used." Programming code does not always provide this; there are certain aspects of a program which are significant but are not part of the operational code. Although some languages have been written so that a reader can interpret the code through the use of common language and clearly defined structures, it is almost always necessary to include with the program information about its development and its control functions. It is estimated that as much as 20% of the development time for commercial software is spent on writing the documentation.

In a comprehensive computer science course, proper attention to documentation is essential. It is unfortunate that most texts that present examples of programming segments almost never include any internal documentation. For the sake of brevity and clarity of the code, almost no explanations are given within the body of the code. Most programs available for student review come from the public domain and are frequently without documentation. (An interesting assignment is to give students a program that is stripped of all documentation, and then to have them document it.)

A programmer should be instilled with the importance of communicating with other programmers and end users, those aspects of the program that are significant but not self-evident. The more creative the programmer, the more important the documentation. The necessity for documentation will be lost on students unless they see good models, and unless they are rewarded for good documentation in their own programming assignments.

Specifications

The first step in documentation of a program is to specify its purpose and function. The specification should include not only a narrative regarding purpose and function, but should also include requirements for input and output.

A teacher can model this aspect of programming in presenting assignments. It not only serves as a good teaching procedure to be very specific in assignments, but a standard approach to assignments will reduce ambiguity and confusion, often sources of management problems in the classroom. Consider the "Assignment Specification" in Figure 3.12. This assignment could be made verbally to the class, or it could be presented in a more condensed narrative form, but headings and a stylized format give students

ASSIGNMENT I
SPECIFICATIONS

Title: Picture-Low Resolution

Function: Prepare a low resolution picture that might
be used as part of a story, a game, or a
front piece for a program.

Files: None

Input: No user input

Output: A low resolution picture (40 × 24 pixels)
with a minimum of three colors, a background setting, and at least one object in
the foreground. One of the objects in the
foreground should have the potential for
movement. (Its "animation" will be considered in another assignment.)

Due: October 1

Figure 3.12. Sample Assignment Specification

a feel for this type of presentation early in a course. As the programming assignments become more complex, the specification
documentation can be modified.

In introductory courses it is unlikely that students are going
to develop their own programs from scratch, so there is little need
or opportunity to teach basic concepts of outlining of specification,
or to become involved in system flowcharting that would be part
of a software development project. It certainly would be worthwhile
to show students examples of the nonprogramming aspects of
software development in order to encourage them to be responsive
to the opportunities to gain more generic communications skills
as part of their training.

Dalbey and Linn (1985, 255), in their review of the requirements
for computer programming, conclude that novices cannot be expected to gain much skill in problem analysis and specifications
during an introductory course, but that does not negate the fact

that this is a skill or phase of programming which requires attention.

External Documentation

In addition to the program specifications, there are two other kinds of documentation that exist outside the program itself: the documentation that describes the data requirements and the operational relationships between the various components of the program. A variety of forms and formats have been developed to assist in presenting an overview of how a program functions, not the least of which are the IPO forms and pseudocode which have already been discussed. Here again, in an introductory course, more elaborate external documentation (HIPOs, structure charts, data-flow diagrams, etc.) may be beyond the scope of the course.

The second type of external documentation deals with the need for the user to have specific, but not necessarily technical information, on how the program works. User manuals are a common form of this kind of documentation.

If there is a trend in documentation it is away from user manuals towards intelligent interfaces, on-line help screens, and user-friendly editors that encourage a user to rely on the capabilities of the computer as an instructional device or tutor and to be less dependent on hardcopy manuals. In the microcomputer environment this is particularly true because of the variety of programs means that a user must have access to a library of manuals which may not be conveniently stored or transported. Nevertheless, a user should have an overall understanding of a program that typically can not be communicated via a computer screen, and there is always the detailed technical information that must be accessible somewhere, sometime—external documentation.

In an introductory course, a user manual is probably unnecessary because most programming assignments are not that complex, but almost any program benefits from hardcopy to introduce the user to its uses and limitations. Again, it is not so much that external documentation is required in an introductory course, but setting a pattern is part of good practice.

Internal Documentation

Internal documentation, unlike external documentation, is not a trivial nor optional matter for the novice. Students have to understand that writing a program must include those aspects of documentation which will make the program serviceable during the writing stage and beyond.

Internal documentation can be viewed as taking place at three levels. To begin with, the individual modules in the program need physical separation from other modules. The use of headings for each module, with a characteristic format that is readily identified, is a beginning. A workable format is shown below.

```
1000  REM
1010  REM    *****************************
1020  REM        MAIN MENU
1030  REM    *****************************
1040  REM
```

At the second level of internal documentation is the narrative that explains the purpose and/or function of a particular module and when appropriate a listing of relevant variables. This level of documentation becomes very important when modules are to be shifted from program to program. The information in this segment is likely to be similar to the information used on the input and output segments of the IPO form. This may seem like an unnecessary duplication, but typically the IPOs are considered only during the development stage of a piece of software, and are not available to the end user. Even if the intent is to provide this information to the end user in hard copy, having the information embedded in the program assures its availability. Having the information within the source code also means that it is available for updating when the source code is updated. One of the lingering problems with external documentation is that it is difficult to update on a continuing basis.

The third level of documentation involves the explanation of particular lines or segments of code. In some cases this may be as minor as defining a variable, while in others it might explain a clever or unique segment of code that the casual or experienced reader might have trouble interpreting. The key here is that at the third level the reader is being assisted in understanding the logic of the code. Obviously the programmer must assume that the reader has some knowledge of the language in which the source code is written, so not every line includes a clarification; but whenever there is doubt, documentation is required.

An example of documentation guidelines for a high school computer science program is presented in Appendix B.

COMMENTARY

The goals of structured programming are to produce programs that will run and meet specifications on their first trial and can be easily modified and maintained. These are also the goals of a computer science teacher, although the rationales might be very different. The computer science teacher hopes that by teaching structured programming the students will gain more generic problem solving skills.

The overriding characteristic of structured programming is that it forces the programmer to be disciplined. The programmer must learn to prepare disciplined code, to incorporate top-down design, to be subject to the careful review process of the walkthrough, and to prepare documentation that is clear and complete. The actual process may vary according to project or organizational needs, but program design, review, coding, and documentation are essential. If the process is followed, programs produced will be reliable, maintainable, and extendible.

Computer science is an evolving discipline, and its guiding principles are encapsulated in the rubrics of structured programming. The techniques have not as yet been codified, but the computer science teacher can incorporate some of the features that experienced programmers agree upon—modules, top-down design, pseudocode, IPOs, walkthroughs—into even introductory courses.

RECOMMENDED READING

Richard J. Weiland, *The Programmer's Craft: Program Construction, Computer Architecture, and Data Management.* Charles R. Bauer (Ed.), Reston Publishing Inc., Reston, Virginia, 1983. A practical guide to the programming task. Full of examples and lists that might otherwise be difficult to find. Good presentation on structured flowcharting.

James Martin and Carma McClure, *Software Maintenance: The Problem and Its Solutions.* Prentice-Hall, Inc., Englewood

Cliffs, New Jersey, 1983. A comprehensive approach to structured programming. Good reference text.

Sally Campell, *Microcomputer Software Design: How to Develop Complex Application Programs*. Prentice-Hall Inc., Englewood Cliffs, New Jersey, 1984. An excellent introduction to structured programming, with the added advantage that it was written for programmers working in the microcomputer environment.

Classics in Software Engineering. Edward Nash Yourdon (Ed.), Yourdon Press, New York, 1979. A compilation of the articles that formed the background for software engineering and structured programming, starting with Dijkstra's landmark paper "Programming Considered as a Human Activity," published in 1965. A depository of papers which provide a historical perspective that will give the computer science teacher an appreciation of computer science as an evolving discipline.

John Dalbey, and Marcia C. Linn, "The Demands and Requirements of Computer Programming: A Literature Review." Journal of Educational Computing Research, Vol. 1, No. 3, 1985, pp. 253–274. A thorough review of the literature; includes references to the professional literature on programming not typically available in the educational journals.

SUGGESTED ACTIVITIES

1. Prepare a short paper on the lives of one of the two pioneers of structured programming, Edsger Dijkstra or Niklaus Wirth.
2. Select one of the following activities and prepare (1) a flowchart; (2) a set of structured flowcharts (Nassi-Shneiderman Diagrams); and (3) a top-down modular plan for it.

- Getting up in the morning.
- Finding a date for Saturday night.
- Fixing a potentially flat tire on your bike.
- Teaching a young child to put away a set of blocks.

3. Prepare a set of masters or transparencies for showing the basic structured flowcharting forms using simple programming modules in either BASIC or Pascal.

CHAPTER 4
INSTRUCTIONAL PROGRAMMING LANGUAGES

Presently there are three programming languages available to the high school computer science teacher—BASIC, LOGO, and Pascal. For each language there is a wide range of versions and adaptations. This chapter provides some background for the selection of a language based on knowledge of its origin, the options available, and the status of the language in the schools. The chapter concludes with a discussion of some of the issues surrounding the programming curriculum.

In this discussion of languages and their implementation, particular attention will be given to the options for the teaching of BASIC, because of its widespread use and the controversy surrounding its lack of structure.

LANGUAGE CHARACTERISTICS

As computer science has developed, choice of an introductory language has been widely discussed and has become a major controversy among teachers of programming. BASIC has become the prevalent language for teaching programming at the high school level, but this may be because BASIC has been the resident language in almost every microcomputer system developed since 1978. The controversy surrounding the use of BASIC as an introductory programming language has focused on its limitations.

The most significant advantage of BASIC as a programming language for microcomputers was that it was very cost-effective, because it required a minimum of memory in its early versions. Although this was a major consideration for those using microcomputers, it did not become a significant factor at the postsecondary level, where college instructors typically had the use of mini-computers or mainframes for instructional purposes.

By the time microcomputers were powerful enough to meet the requirements of college instruction, other languages were available on the microcomputer. Introductory courses at the college level had evolved to the point that Pascal was preferred as the first programming language, especially for students planning to make computer science a career.

The fact that Pascal is preferred at the college level has not been lost on high school teachers, but the movement to Pascal is limited by a number of factors. Aside from BASIC's general availability, it has little else to offer as a programming language. But for most high school teachers the switch to Pascal would mean a costly investment in further education; in fact, their entire approach to the teaching of programming might have to be reexamined. These are not easy changes because they involve a significant time commitment from an instructor who is more than likely already overextended by the demands of being a computer science teacher.

The bright side of the picture is the fact that Pascal has been identified as the Advanced Placement language, and the qualities of Pascal that have endeared it to the college instructors are being used as guidelines by those developing precollege instruction. The dominance of BASIC as the most common language and the enthusiasm for LOGO as a language that teaches problem-solving skills has kept the issue of language in introductory courses an open question.

As a starting point in the selection of an introductory computer language, the following guidelines may be helpful:

- Can the language be used to teach the concepts considered necessary for good programming form and style: that is, structured or procedural programming?
- Is the language compatible with those languages students are likely to meet in more advanced courses?
- Does the student have the cognitive skills required to understand and use the language?
- Is the language usable on hardware that will not become obsolete in the immediate future?
- Is the cost of providing sufficient legal copies of the programming language for all students and/or workstations reasonable?

- How much instructional time will be required for the student to master the use of the editor?

It is important to consider the selection of a programming language in some detail, as it is likely that computer science teachers will begin their careers as the first in the school with any formal training in computer science. They may be called upon to choose a language, or find themselves in a position of needing to develop a curriculum around a language which has been selected for them. In either case, it will be helpful to know more than a single language, and more than just the syntax of the language.

At one time there was a movement to make BASIC the standard language for high school instruction. The National Council of Teachers of Mathematics recommended BASIC as the standard language back in 1966 (Time-Life 1986, 99), when BASIC was almost the only language available; this was at a time when programming was being taught on a very limited basis. The availability and potential of the microcomputer were not envisioned.

More than 20 years later, Luehrmann's (1982) view is probably still the most viable; there is no "right" computer language. A language and how it is taught must be viewed with regard to the goals and objectives that have been set for the particular students. Certainly there will be different needs and expectations among different groups of students.

Masterson (1984) has suggested that selection of a programming language for beginners should be based on certain qualities of the language. He proposed the following criteria for the selection of a computing language for an introductory course:

- Simplicity—The language needs to be simple enough that students can learn to solve simple problems.
- Power—It must, however, have the capacity to solve complicated problems.
- Compatibility—The language should not be so unique that it is not compatible with other computer languages or applications.
- Cognitive Richness—Learning the language should facilitate thinking about various problems in terms of data representations and structures.

In the discussion illustrating these guidelines, Masterson used ALGOL, FORTRAN, Pascal, LOGO, LISP and BASIC to show how these concepts might apply. Masterson was arguing at the time for his own language—AMPL, a modified version of APL—so some bias and selectivity might have been involved in developing his list. Nevertheless, the criteria are worthy of note; as time goes on, the choice of an introductory language will become even more complex as more powerful systems and greater choices become available in the pre-college environment.

An important consideration in the selection of a programming language for naive students is the choice of an editor. Unlike the sophisticated systems and tools available on minicomputers and mainframes, editors on microcomputers can be very limited. Currently, the demands placed on the memory available in typical microcomputers severely inhibits implementation with all the "bells and whistles" that might be desired. This situation is changing as memory continues to become less expensive, and computers with sixteen and thirty-two bit data buses become available and affordable. Meanwhile, the problem remains that on the individual workstations that high school teachers typically use there is a real need to consider the editor. Probably as much thought needs to go into this decision as into the selection of the programming language. Without a good editor, students spend an inordinate amount of time correcting code instead of working on planning and problem solving.

Teachers with limited experience may not be aware of the difference a good editor can make. Simple conveniences like automatic line numbering or highlighting of syntactical errors can be very helpful when working with naive students. Even experienced students have trouble moving back and forth between the editor and the run modes, between the library and the workspace, and between the source code and the compiled program. In some cases when students claim they cannot learn programming, the difficulty may be with the editor.

Authors of computer languages are aware of the problems that editors present for naive users, but often the writers are not teachers and what they consider simple concepts may present almost insurmountable problems to some students. For example, anyone who tries to introduce LOGO to primary level children quickly realizes that the students have trouble distinguishing between the edit mode and the run mode. This level of abstraction can present a major learning obstacle in a language which was supposedly written for young children. Of course, thoughtful teachers have found ways to get around this obstacle and there have been many successful implementations of LOGO, but LOGO will be more successful when the editing is made more transparent and user friendly.

When choosing a particular version of a programming language, a good rule of thumb would be: *"The editor should be easier to learn than the language that is being taught."*

BASIC

One of the few languages written specifically for beginning programmers is BASIC (Beginners All-purpose Symbolic Instructional Code). It is clearly the dominant language at the high school level. According to the recent national survey of computer coordinators (Martinez and Mead 1988), 91.9% of the high school coordinators felt prepared to teach BASIC, while only 35.4% felt prepared to teach LOGO and 35.8% to teach Pascal. There are many reasons for the dominance of BASIC, not the least of which has been its availability as the resident language on the ubiquitous microcomputer. It has been essentially free to the purchaser of almost any microcomputer.

In addition to the economic factors, BASIC is typically an interpreted language on the microcomputer, and therefore an easy language to work with, although the "quick and dirty" approach is not without its problems. Line-by-line writing of programs leads to editing and adapting programs with little concern for form or style. BASIC, as a language, does not require the discipline of a procedural language, and this can lead to programming which is unnecessarily complex and convoluted. On the positive side, being able to write partial programs, or having programs run line-by-line until a fatal error is detected, can be motivating to the novice. Teaching a compiled language to a novice makes one quickly aware of the need for at least partial success in the early programming sessions, something not always easily achieved.

Much of the debate about the value of BASIC has focused on its lack of internal structure. It has been said that a student who is taught BASIC may be actually hindered in his learning of other languages because certain bad habits become so entrenched that they can not be "untaught." The most severe critic of BASIC is Dijkstra, who is considered by some to be the father of structured programming. He has suggested that learning BASIC can be damaging. Dijkstra has been quoted (Garland 1984) as saying:

"It is practically impossible to teach good programming to students that have had a prior exposure to BASIC; as potential programmers they are mentally mutilated beyond hope of regeneration."

This opinion must be considered an extreme statement, but it has fueled the debate over the efficacy of BASIC as an instructional programming language.

The more moderate response to the lack of a disciplined programming style in BASIC has been the argument that the language itself does not lead to the convoluted and unintelligible code, frequently referred to as "spaghetti code." Those who write the code are at fault. If computer science teachers understand the importance of structured programming, they will insist that form and style be as important to their students as execution of programs. The same issues do not surface with respect to LOGO and Pascal because the procedural nature of these languages tends to prevent unstructured programming.

The problems with BASIC are not limited to matters of style. Most versions of BASIC at the high school level have built-in limitations. In order to prepare a programming language that will work in an environment limited to 64 K of memory, certain tradeoffs have been made. We will look at the various approaches to providing students with a structured approach to programming in the "unstructured" BASIC environment in Appendix C.

If the guidelines suggested by Masterson (1984) are applied, BASIC can be rated as fairly high on simplicity because even beginning students can be taught to write programs within a hour or so that solve general types of numeric or string manipulation problems. On the power scale, BASIC may not be the favorite of academic programmers, but it is still the most popular language for the microcomputer programmer because it can be used for programs in the business environment. The large number of programs written in BASIC for microcomputers give it a high rating in terms of compatibility. The weakness of the language is probably most evident when cognitive richness is considered. BASIC does not usually provide a full range of data structures, local and global variables, and recursion; all features that suggest approaches to solving problems which utilize the power and creative capacity of the computer.

This is not to suggest that BASIC is an unsuitable language; all languages have their limitations. There are always tradeoffs in the development of a language. In response to BASIC's weakness in cognitive richness, it can be argued that the language is rich enough for an introductory language, especially if the limitations can be offset by careful instruction in format and style.

In general, the limitations of many of the common versions of BASIC are reduced by adopting rules of format and style to make the language at least resemble more powerful and cognitively rich languages. Some of these approaches will be described with samples of code in Appendix C in order to give a sense of what is meant when it is suggested that there is a need to teach "structured BASIC."

BASIC: Background

● Dartmouth: The initial development of BASIC was done at Dartmouth College in the early sixties by Kemeny and Kurtz (1985). They were motivated by the need to have a language that students could use to interact with a computer, a language that would require only a few hours to learn. They had hoped that the language could be learned in three hours or less. The design of the language included the following features:

1. It should be easy to learn for the beginner.
2. It should be a general-purpose language, allowing the writing of any program.
3. When an advanced feature had to be added, if there was a price, it was to be paid by the expert, not the novice.
4. It should take full advantage of the fact that the user could interact directly with the computer.
5. It should give error messages that were clear and friendly to the user.
6. It should give fast response for small programs.
7. The user should not have to understand the hardware.
8. The system should shield the user from the operating system. (P9)

Out of these humble beginnings came the most popular computer language of all time. The original operational level of BASIC was limited to 14 commands, and was a compiled version. Even at this level, it was widely used because it was the first interactive language, and it was coupled to the development of a time-sharing system which enhanced the real-time use of computers. Between

1963 and 1971, seven versions of BASIC were produced at Dartmouth; each version gaining in sophistication and power, but never forgetting that the language was designed for beginners.

The original versions of BASIC developed at Dartmouth were placed in the public domain and were available to all interested parties. BASIC was widely used and developed as hardware became more and more available. The release to the public meant that anyone who wanted to could change or modify the language to meet their own needs. This adaptability lead to many versions and dialects, which contributed to a lack of compatibility among versions of BASIC, which has persisted. The original BASIC was developed on a mainframe computer.

• Tiny BASIC: When it became apparent that a computer language for the microcomputer was necessary, one of the most novel responses was the contest conducted by People's Computer Company. Dennis Allison wrote a series of articles suggesting what a minimum interpreter might be like for the Altair 8800, and invited his readers to produce the interpreter. The result was Tiny BASIC. The original response was 20 pages of octal code—some 2000 octal-code instructions—which needed to be loaded through toggle switches. This took as long as three hours to load, and was lost when the computer was turned off.

The unexpected interest in the language quickly lead to the development of a new journal, Dr. Dobb's Journal of Tiny BASIC Calisthenics & Orthodontia: Running Light without Overbyte which eventually evolved into Dr. Dobb's Journal of Computers. Interest spread as more and more microcomputers became available. Many versions of Tiny BASIC were produced and distributed by enthusiastic hobbyists. For the most part, computer programming on microcomputers was viewed as a sharing activity, and there was little interest in commercial applications. Information was freely exchanged between those promoting the use of microcomputers.

• Microsoft BASIC: The first commercial computer, the Altair 8800, was marketed by Micro Instrumentation and Telemetry Systems (MITS) in 1975 and with it was marketed its own version of BASIC which had been developed by Bill Gates and Paul Allen. This version sold for $500, and it was the precursor of the most popular of all BASICs, Microsoft BASIC. The appearance of a commercial form of BASIC initiated the debate about the efficacy of commercial and public domain software.

BASIC was the language of choice by manufacturers of almost

all microcomputers. Not only was the language easy to learn, but it could be incorporated into the limited memory space available in the first microcomputers. When a computer was limited to 48 or 64K of memory, the options for a programming language were highly restricted. The versions of BASIC that were developed for the microcomputer tended to be minimum adaptations. According to Kemeny and Kurtz (1985, 20), the microcomputer versions were based on an early version of Dartmouth BASIC and tended to overlook modifications that had been in place at Dartmouth for several years. They suggest that many of the criticisms of BASIC as a programming language are due to the tradeoffs made in developing microcomputer versions, and they are therefore not valid for BASIC as it is implemented on mainframes and minicomputers.

• ANSI BASIC: The American National Standards Institute (ANSI) in 1974 established a committee to propose a standard for the BASIC language. Their original product was a standard called ANSI Minimal BASIC which organized the progeny of the original Dartmouth BASIC that were proliferating in the microcomputer environment. According to Luehrmann (1984d), Minimal BASIC is not truly a language but an attempt to find the common elements of the various dialects already in use.

The original work of the committee was expanded into a true standard which includes the elements of top-down design, modules, and control structures. ANSI BASIC (ANSI X3.113-1987) is a dialect rather than a super version of BASIC; it sets some requirements for versions in the future. Some examples from the standards are:

1. Line numbers are an option for the programmer.
2. Uppercase and lowercase letters are equivalent except as string constants.
3. Variable names are not limited in length.
4. Local variables are the rule, not the exception.
5. Variables can be transferred back and forth in the form of parameters.

All future versions of BASIC will be gauged according to how well they meet the rules and requirements set in the ANSI standard.

• True BASIC: In 1984, Kemeny and Kurtz reviewed the status of BASIC, and decided to prepare a version that was not hampered by the compromises of their earlier version at Dartmouth. In fact, the version of BASIC that has been used at Dartmouth already had incorporated many elements of the ANSI standard in the twenty years since its original edition, but the more popular version published by Microsoft was based on the early, and more primitive, version of BASIC. Their new version is called True BASIC (Kemeny and Kurtz 1987).

True BASIC takes into account the standards developed by ANSI, and incorporates principles of structured programming. The editor includes features which detect some syntactical errors during the writing of code, and the interpreter-compiler was designed to make transportability between different makes and models of machines easier to execute.

True BASIC is not the only ANSI version available. Microsoft has a version called Quick BASIC (1987); Borland has Turbo BASIC (1986); and Summit Software has Better BASIC (1984). The latter three versions are not available for the Apple. Hertzberg (1987) has prepared a short review of all four versions that might prove informative for anyone considering the purchase of one or the other of the four.

BASIC: Options

The development of BASIC as a language has not been a simple linear progression. The language has not been taken as a serious computer language by those who were leading the profession; in fact, the language has been treated as a minor player in a rapidly growing field. Languages were being developed to respond to serious needs of business, government and the scientific community. Nevertheless, without the support of the computer scientists, the language became widely known to the general public.

It is estimated that by 1980, over eight million people had learned to program in BASIC, and the number continues to grow as rapidly as microcomputers spread throughout the various business and educational environments. It is clearly the common man's language of choice.

With all this activity, it is not surprising that various forms and dialects of the language have spread. In part this was due to the various microcomputers having different operating systems, and even though many of them used a form of Microsoft BASIC, different versions were required for different hardware systems.

Instead of trying to inventory the numerous versions of BASIC, we will look instead at a selected group of options that have been developed specifically to overcome problems associated with the unstructured nature of the language. This material can be found in Appendix C: Structuring BASIC. An introductory text, for the pre-college environment using a structured approach to BASIC is the popular Computer Literacy—A Hands-On Approach (Luehrmann and Peckham 1986).

BASIC: Status

Just because BASIC has been taught without structure in the past does not mean it has to be taught that way in the future. As we have just seen, there are methods for teaching BASIC which can equip the student with all the most important principles of structured programming. Taught from principles rather than "whatever works," BASIC may have more potential than its past record would indicate.

There is a body of research being developed concerning the problems encountered when teaching programming. What is interesting is that the same problems occur whether the language is Pascal or BASIC. This could indicate the beginnings of a coherent pedagogical theory.

LOGO

The main challenge to BASIC as the principal introductory language is LOGO. A phenomenon of the eighties was the following that developed around the teaching of LOGO. National and international conferences bring together people for the sole purpose of developing and promoting the language. It is estimated that forty thousand teachers are using LOGO in their classrooms (Becker 1987). The most interesting thing is that there is considerable debate about the value of LOGO as a programming language.

LOGO: Background

• Artificial Intelligence Laboratory at MIT: In the mid and late sixties, Seymour Papert and colleagues at MIT undertook to develop a system that would make it possible for children to interact with a computer. The original goal was to determine how they learn from the experience. Using LISP, a procedural language being developed to simulate how the mind works, as the parent language, Papert and his associates created a new language and a unique learning environment in which students teach the computer how to do things.

The early experiments included a robot tethered to a mainframe computer. The children, working independently, were given geometric problems to solve and they directed the robot to act out their solutions. Through careful observation and analysis, a very powerful, yet simple, language emerged.

The findings of the MIT group led to the publication of possibly the most significant book in educational computing Mindstorms (Papert 1980). This book has attracted the attention of a great number of teachers, and has served as a rallying point for a group of advocates of teaching programming to young children.

• Terrapin and Apple LOGO: The LOGO language was adopted for the microcomputer in the early eighties and on the basis of the rationale presented in Mindstorms, LOGO became the educational software innovation of the early eighties, just as the Apple II was the hardware sensation of the late seventies.

The lackluster attempts to instruct teachers in BASIC were quickly overshadowed by the welcome given to LOGO in the elementary school. The acceptance of LOGO has not been without its critics, and a somewhat more tempered view of its credibility has now developed in the educational community (Moursund 1986).

LOGO was accepted by elementary school teachers, and its procedural power was apparent to computer science teachers. It is argued that LOGO is a better introductory language than BASIC, and many teachers have replaced BASIC with LOGO.

• LogoWriter: An interesting innovation in the evolution of LOGO has been the development of LogoWriter (1986). This implementation of LOGO has combined the turtle graphics, for which LOGO is so well known, with a word processor. The idea is to capitalize on the graphics capabilities of LOGO in order to enhance the creative aspects of the word processor. Although some of the primitives in the original LOGO have been removed, LogoWriter provides an integrated package with both a programming environment and a word processor. For many teachers, the tradeoffs that were necessary to build a word processor may not be apparent, but neither lengthy LOGO programs nor lengthy documents can be handled. The maximum document size is four thousand characters.

LogoWriter may be the start of a trend away from LOGO as a

programming language to LOGO as a teaching utility or a learning environment.

LOGO: Options

According to Harvey (1987) there are fourteen currently available versions of LOGO; four versions for the Apple II series and five for the IBM PC. There is at least one for each of the popular computers, and a recent interest in Macintosh versions. The earlier versions of LOGO followed either of two approaches: LOGO Computer Systems, Inc. or Terrapin, Inc. Although similar in most respects these two approaches use different sets of syntax rules. Harvey provides an excellent discussion on the differences.

The newer versions of LOGO for the Macintosh include features that are unique. The Macintosh has provided the language designer the opportunity to include some features that had to be removed from the original LOGO as designed for MIT's mainframe and to add features not envisioned at that time. ExperProLogo by ExperTelligence, for example, includes speech primitives and three-dimensional graphics, and Object LOGO uses an object-oriented approach, making LOGO a valid option for some commercial applications.

LOGO: Status

Although LOGO as a language is a viable tool for the computer science teacher, teaching it is not as simple as some would have us believe. According to Moursund (1986), to be a good LOGO instructor, one must have knowledge of problem solving, discovery-based learning, and individualization of instruction. One must also understand the hardware and software requirements of the language.

LOGO is a very popular program; according to LOGO Computer Systems, Inc., as reported by Khayrallah and Meiraker (1987), around 150,000 copies of LOGO have been sold for the Apple II computer. As cited earlier, Becker (1986) estimates that in 1985, more than 40,000 teachers were using LOGO in their classes, amounting to about 9% of all computer-using teachers. Three quarters of these teachers taught in grades K-5. More than 25% of elementary teachers who use computers employ LOGO. Although these percentages are quite significant, it should be noted that the same survey showed that most teachers were using LOGO to supplement or enrich their curriculum rather than for a separate part of their regular instructional program.

What this data suggests is that despite the cost, LOGO is widely available to teachers and it is being used. Teachers are finding something of value in LOGO and adapting it to meet their own needs and style. Thus, it has found a place in the computer-using classroom.

This acceptance is not to be interpreted as meaning that there are no problems with LOGO. The research on LOGO is not as supportive as might be expected, considering its origins and early reports on its successes. Issues surrounding the use of LOGO as an instructional programming language are discussed later in this chapter.

The commercial success of LOGO may be a force that will keep it a viable programming language. The newer computers, the Apple GS and the Macintosh, have capabilities for more user-friendly environments for teaching LOGO, as well as tools that can bring the full range of functions into common use. It remains to be seen how the newer editions will impact a typical classroom.

PASCAL

Long before the issue of which computer language would be the best for the elementary or high school student emerged, computer science teachers in the colleges and universities were confronted with the same question, but their needs were quite different. As computing machines increased in number and complexity during the sixties, so did the languages which were designed or modified to match them. In 1969, Jean Sammet published the first comprehensive survey of computer languages, and identified 117 different ones. Considering that in the early 1960s there were, for all practical purposes, only three languages—FORTRAN, COBOL and ALGOL 60—this amounted to a major outpouring of creative work, and presented a major problem for those preparing computer scientists.

Languages were being designed to solve specific types of problems, and others were being written for specific hardware. During the sixties, general purpose languages were giving way to special purpose languages, and instruction at the university level was becoming impossible. It was necessary to teach general concepts and principles without being tied to a general purpose language or a specific hardware system. Out of this milieu, Niklaus Wirth designed Pascal, a language for teaching the theory and techniques of programming.

Pascal: Background

Niklaus Wirth's training was in electrical engineering, and he designed his language in the same way that an engineer might design a machine. His approach to programming (Wirth 1984) is that the process is analogous to taking a general purpose machine, and through the use of the language, designing another machine which will do a specific task. The Wirth article makes interesting reading because it conveys the point of view that produced the first language requiring a structured approach.

The "machine-like" language needs to be made up of independent parts which the programmer can select and order as needed. The construction of the machine requires a set of rules, but the rules should not interfere with operation of the machine. The result of this approach was Pascal. Pascal is a very formal language, a language that is capable of producing very logical and elequent code. The language was exactly what was needed to teach the concepts of structured programming being proposed at the time by the programming theorists.

Despite its early limitation for the production of commercial software, Pascal was widely adopted by colleges and universities as their language of preference for teaching computer science students.

- UCSD Pascal: One of the early versions of Pascal was developed at the University of California at San Diego. This particular version was written in an attempt to make Pascal more portable between machines. The programming language took the source code and compiled it into an intermediate form which was then run using an interpreter. This was an unusual approach. Someone would write a program using the proper Pascal syntax, and the program would then be compiled—this is typical of most versions of Pascal—but after it is compiled, the compiled version is run using an interpreter to produce the machine code.

The advantage of this arrangement is that the same version of the language can be used on any machine, provided that an interpreter is written for that machine. The concept was identified as using a p-code interpreter (p-code stands for pseudo-machine code). This innovation made the language very portable at a time when people were concerned about preparing software for one computer and then having to start virtually from scratch to produce a version for a different computer. Pascal became popular with programmers designing software for small systems.

One of the earliest versions of Pascal for the microcomputer was Apple's UCSD Pascal. Using the modular concept of Pascal, it was possible to develop a sophisticated system of editor, library programs, compiler and interpreter, to be used on a 64K Apple or 64K IBM-PC. Teachers had an alternative to BASIC as a programming language to be taught on a microcomputer.

Pascal on a 64K computer is not without its problems. With an operating system as complex as that of the Pascal system, a complicated process of exchanging disks and program segments is necessary in order to leave a usable amount of workspace available for the source program. This complicates the teaching of programming because not only do students spend a great deal of time manipulating disks, but they also become confused about what is and what is not available to them in working on the system. UCSD Pascal might be an excellent version when used on a minicomputer with all the support systems on line, but as a programming language for a microcomputer the Apple version was an example of an implementation in which the editor was more difficult to learn than the language itself.

• Advanced Placement Computer Science: In 1983, a task force of the College Board presented its recommendation (Braswell 1984) for an Advanced Placement course of study which selected Pascal to be the sole language for the advanced placement examination being offered in the spring of 1984. The task force made the recommendation on the choice of language after 3 years of study. Because many high school computer science teachers were not knowledgeable about the language and did not have the background to cover the range of topics on the examination, the recommendation was somewhat controversial.

Despite misgivings of the high school teachers on the task force concerning the efficacy of the decision, the awarding of college credit for a high school course required that the course meet the criteria established at the college level and the college representatives carried the day. This decision has probably done more to standardize the offerings of high school courses than any other. It will certainly ensure the teaching of Pascal at the precollege level.

It should be noted that an Advanced Placement course is not

be construed as meaning that the committee was recommending that Pascal should be the only, even the preferred, course for high school students. The committee pointed out that the course was not intended to replace or influence courses already being used to introduce secondary school students to computing. Advanced Placement courses should be viewed as extensions of the standard curriculum which provide capable students the opportunity to do advanced work in the high school setting. Nevertheless, the course of study (Appendix D) recommended by the College Board articulated those aspects of computer science which were to be considered the primary content of the subject matter, and the concepts are essentially language-independent.

The following summary typifies the rationale for selecting Pascal:

> The language must have certain technical characteristics that facilitate structured programming and a high degree of modularity, for example, the *if-then-else-* flow construct, the *while-do* looping construct, data typing, and independent procedures. These procedures must allow the use of parameters, declaration of local variables, and access to global variables. It should be possible to pass parameters both by reference and by value. Recursion and dynamic allocation of storage are also necessary features (Braswell 1984, 375).

The committee was quick to point out that Pascal was not the only language which had these features, but for the immediate future it was their recommendation that the test be restricted to Pascal because it was the only language which was widely available for the high school classroom.

● Instant Pascal: The editing problems with Pascal on a microcomputer were resolved when Pascal was introduced on the Macintosh. The Macintosh environment provided editing features that went beyond those commonly found on minicomputers. Pull-down menus, multiple windows, and a mouse added dimensions to the editor and contributed to the ease of programming.

These same features were incorporated in an interpreted version of Pascal that was subsequently developed for the Apple II with 128K of memory—Instant Pascal. Not only did Instant Pascal have many features of more advanced computers, it had an editor that would flag syntax errors, and an instant window which would allow the programmer to test out small segments of programs before incorporating them into the main program. The graphics capacities were similar to the Macintosh, and it had the added feature of color.

Pascal: Options

Unlike BASIC and LOGO, Pascal is a well-defined language with prescribed rules and syntax. Variations between different versions of the language are relatively minor. The options available to the instructor are decided more on the basis of available hardware than on minor variations in implementation.

• Apple II: If all that is available are Apple II computers, the obvious choice would be Instant Pascal (see above), although some schools may have too much invested in Apple Pascal or lack 128K machines and need to contend with the frustration of the USCD editor and p-code.

• Apple IIGS: There are two Pascal compilers—Orca Pascal from the Byte Works and TML Pascal from TML Systems—for the Apple GS computer which take advantage of many Macintosh-like features including the use of the desktop concept and the mouse. Although the actual language differences are small, and both systems are compiled rather than interpreted, there are some significant differences between these two versions both in operation and editing. A thorough discussion of these differences can be found in an article by Fischer (1988).

• Macintosh: If Macintoshes are used to teach Pascal, there is a version that uses an interactive interpreter offered by Apple— Macintosh Pascal. It is a full implementation of Pascal and it comes very close to meeting the ANSI standard. In addition, it supports the graphics functions of the Macintosh Quickdraw program, and an innovative editing tool, Instant Window. Within the window, small program segments can be entered, edited and executed; this should be a very useful educational tool.

• IBM (MS-DOS): The most popular version of Pascal is Borland International's Turbo Pascal for the IBM. Its popularity is due to its low cost which was achieved without decreasing power and speed. Early versions of Turbo Pascal had a serious memory limitation in that maximum program size was set at 64K. This limitation has been removed in version 4.0 by the utilization of 64K modules. It has very extensive on-line documentation.

In addition to Turbo Pascal, there are at least four other versions of Pascal available—MS-Pascal, UCSD Pascal, Pro Pascal and

Professional Pascal. These versions differ in the ways they handle linkage, debugging, compiling, data types, program components and other special features. Many of the differences would only be of significance to those involved in very sophisticated or large scale software development projects. Choosing among the options would require detailed analysis of the specific needs of a programmer, and a consultation with a review, such as the one provided by Shammas (1986), in which four versions are compared. Some of the advanced features do not concern the instructor in an introductory course, and in fact might complicate instruction for novice programmers by providing too many options.

Pascal: Status

A new computer science teacher must be careful about viewing the comments and criticisms of early versions of Pascal as applying to versions available today. Many earlier opinions were due to the complications inherent in the editors of the time, and the editors were limited by available memory. The problems were, and are, not with Pascal as a language, but more in the way it had to be taught on computers with limited memories.

Over the years, Pascal has developed into an acceptable professional language, and it is frequently used in commercial applications. Pascal is clearly the language of choice among college instructors, although Modula-2, C and LISP have their advocates.

THE CURRICULUM

Although computers have been in schools in significant numbers for a relatively short time, the curriculum has gone through a rapid series of changes. In a recent analysis of the computer's changing role in the schools, Norton (1988) documented the following trends or models: The Programming Curriculum, The Computer Literacy Curriculum, The Computer as Tool Curriculum, The Problem-Solving Computer Curriculum, and the Integrated Curricular Model. The computer science teacher will surely incorporate elements of each of these into his own courses of study, but the present wisdom is that the goal of teaching programming, or computer science in its broadest sense, is to develop problem-solving skills.

This text is written on the assumption that programming is a viable component of the curriculum and can be taught in such a way as to develop problem-solving skills. However, the computer science teacher should be aware of the alternative approaches for teaching problem solving, and for using computers to serve other goals of the schools.

Problem Solving

The power of the computer to engage a student's attention along with recognition that it is a useful tool for problem solving in business and industry is well-established. This view has naturally led to the proposition that the computer environment is a logical place to teach problem-solving skills. This supposition has been further extrapolated to the point that it is argued that computer related problem-solving skills are best taught by teaching students to program. The wide acceptance of the goal of teaching students to be problem solvers is hardly in dispute, but the meaning of the term "problem solving" is almost as ambiguous as the term "computer literacy."

The process of programming clearly involves a number of identifiable components of problem solving: identifying the problem, reducing the problem to manageable components, building separate components into a total solution, testing, debugging, validating etc. But an issue remains: is the programming environment the proper or productive one for teaching problem-solving skills, or are there better approaches to teaching problem solving with the computer?

The novel and engaging qualities of the medium have led to a variety of stimulating programs which challenge students without the necessity of teaching them to program. Simulations are one impressive use of the computer in the school setting.

The issue of teaching children problem-solving skills via programming and/or using the computer has become involved in the larger debate about teaching higher order thinking skills. Most observers of our schools agree that little is being done that would qualify as teaching children to be problem solvers. The evidence indicates that the development and transfer of problem-solving skills through schooling is very limited. The research on transfer of problem-solving skills or cognitive development has tended to focus on the teaching of LOGO. This topic is receiving a great deal of attention in the literature.

One of the most widely discussed studies of the effect of programming on children's thinking was done by Clements and Gullo (1984). Working with eighteen six-year-olds, they showed that significant differences were obtained on measures of reflectivity, divergent thinking, measures of metacognitive ability and the ability to describe directions when compared to a control group that received an equivalent amount of computer-assisted instruction.

A second study by Clements (1986) with first and third graders showed similar results for specific cognitive skills (classification and seriation), metacognitive skills, creativity, and knowledge of directions. The results of the two experiments were not completely consistent, but the slight differences in outcomes could be attributed to slight modifications in treatment; the second experiment incorporated less direct teaching and more independent study.

Other attempts to ascertain the effectiveness of programming on transfer of problem solving have met with less success. In a well-known study, Pea and Kurland (1984) showed that LOGO students did not do better than a control group with respect to a planning task. In this particular example, 32 students who had participated in 30 hours of instruction in LOGO were compared to a no-treatment control group on a planning task. The LOGO students showed no particular skill in the planning task. A replication of the study involving more programming and a computer-based evaluation failed to yield positive findings on transfer. The question that continues to be raised is: why did the Clements work show significant changes in cognitive skills, while the Pea studies showed no gains for a somewhat simpler task?

Salomon and Perkins (1987) suggest that the differences in the results between the Clements and Pea studies of transfer of problem-solving skills occur because transfer of problem-solving skills depends a great deal on the kind of skill that is transferred. In one approach, the instruction focuses on a target skill which is closely related to the skill demonstrated in instruction. When the instructional skill and the target skill have similar or common elements, the transfer would be identified as "low road" and the transfer would depend to a large degree on the amount of drill and practice of the instructional skill.

In the second type of transfer, the instructional skill is only used as an example of a more generic skill, and the instruction calls upon the student to recognize and understand the general idea. This process is called "high road" transfer, and it is characterized by reflection and articulation of the process involved in the skill. The learner is taught to make deliberate, mindful abstractions when addressing a problem to see if it holds common elements with other known, solvable problems or approaches. The problem solver is challenged to articulate or symbolize the plan or principle in an effort to identify attributes amenable to more abstract considerations. Salomon and Perkins suggest that either or both approaches to utilizing programming for learning generic problem-solving skills "might" be possible.

Not only do students have to receive specific training if they are to develop transferable skills, but the planning of instruction, the curriculum, should take into account the kinds of skills to be transferred. In their analysis, Salomon and Perkins (1987) suggest six broad categories of transfer relative to programming:

1. Mathematical and Geometric Concepts and Principles
2. Problem Solving, Problem Finding, and Problem Management Strategies
3. Abilities of Formal Reasoning and Representation
4. Models of Knowledge, Thinking, and Learning
5. Cognitive Styles
6. Enthusiasms and Tolerances

They further suggest that there are opportunities for both low- and high-level transfer of problem-solving skills within each of these categories, and although the categories are not mutually exclusive, and may be quite different for the expert and novice programmer, they indicate more than a general concept or model for problem solving.

On a post hoc basis, they examined the studies of Clements and Gullo (1984) and Clements (1986) in which positive transfer effects were reported. Although there was no explicit design for instruction in transfer, both studies included elements which paralleled those that might have been used had they been designed to practice high road transfer. For example, the treatment included adult tutors who encouraged students to think aloud about the programming process.

The lack of transfer in the Kurland, Pea, Clement, and Mawby (1986) studies is also consistent with the requirements for low road transfer. The planning task was developed because it was thought to parallel the types of tasks the students experienced in their programming. But the students, as the authors noted, had minimal programming skills. Low road transfer requires a high level of performance in the primary area before transfer can be mapped into common elements in the nonprogramming context. Salomon and Perkins (1987) also point out that the original authors did not make explicit reference to instruction in abstracting and bridging activities which would have been necessary for high road transfer.

In a review of Linn's 1985 study, Salomon and Perkins point to the evidence of low road transfer of programming skills from BASIC to an instructional language called "Spider World." The twenty-four students for this study were selected from a population of 2400 students based on their apparent high ability. Twenty-one of the students had received instruction from a single, exemplary teacher who required students to examine their own work before receiving help and who employed "guided discovery techniques to help students reformulate code." (1985, 26) These students may have met the prerequisite of high programming performance.

Although the latter study tends to add credibility to the notion that transfer of problem-solving skills can be characterized in terms of the desired outcomes, the analysis is disconcerting. It suggests that low road transfer requires a high level of programming expertise. What is disconcerting is that this is unlikely to occur considering the demands on the resources of the schools and the lack of sustaining interest and availability of programming instruction. The lack of well-taught students seems to be a problem even in schools that are confident enough in their programs to allow outside researchers to observe and collect data. Surprisingly, the potential for high road transfer is better. Through the use of better instructional strategies which involve planned mediating tactics, transfer may occur and general cognitive skills may be improved.

Keep in mind, the model proposed by Salomon and Perkins (1987) is very speculative, and the research evidence offered in support of the conjecture is limited, selective, and was analyzed on a post hoc basis. Even more disturbing than the analysis of the low/high road model is that the universal claim that programming will improve a student's problem-solving skills has no firm research base; at this point in time it is more a matter of speculation than fact.

More recently, research by Black, Swan and Schwartz (1988) showed that when specific problem-solving strategies are taught using various LOGO contextual grouping—turtle graphics, list manipulation, and combined turtle graphics and list manipulation— there were significant gains in specific problem-solving skills. This research is encouraging. It suggests that when specific skills are identified as outcomes, and when the instruction is matched to these outcomes, programming can be effective in teaching problem solving. This study supports the low road hypothesis because the students were taught specific strategies to solve specific types of problems.

The instruction in the research by Black et al. was designed for students who were not only familiar with LOGO, the programming language, but old enough to be capable of formal thought—Grades 4 through 8. The problem-solving strategies were also selected because they were considered useful for children of this age range. The strategies were subgoals formation, forward-chaining, backward-chaining, systematic trial and error, alternative problem representation, and analogical reasoning. Backward-chaining was the only strategy which did not prove to yield a significant pre-post test difference after three months of instruction (two 45-minute periods a week).

Overall, the research studies suggest a potential for programming as a way of developing cognitive skills when it is taught with a view toward transfer and bridging. But the research is less than conclusive, and it is subject to many interpretations. The problem is exacerbated by the fact that many who work on the research are so anxious to see positive results they may be unwilling to ask the serious questions. All but the most myopic would agree that there is a discontinuity between the anticipated and the observed effects of programming.

One of the more thoughtful reviews of the literature is that of Johanson. (1988) He approaches the disparity with the pragmatic view that even if we cannot demonstrate that programming leads to the positive cognitive consequences, programming should not be excluded from the curriculum any more than any other subject which lacks a research base. Curricular analysis should be the tool for making decisions about instructional strategies, and this analysis is typically based on professional judgment and intuition as much as on experimental research. Johanson proposed the following hypotheses:

1. A cognitive chain of consequences exists; students are not progressing to the end of the chain, but could.
2. Applications represent a more likely arena than programming in which to look for the desired cognitive outcomes.
3. The research on cognitive outcomes of programming has been poorly conceptualized.

4. Research has been unsophisticated and done at the wrong age level.
5. The anticipation of cognitive benefits constitutes a resurrection of the discredited concept of mental discipline.
6. Problem solving, higher-order thinking, divergent thinking and other goals of programming instruction are discontinuous with the regular curriculum and unlikely to be achieved.
7. Problem-solving and higher-order thinking may be domain-specific.
8. Failure to find the desired effects of programming, such as higher-order thinking, problem solving, and enhanced meta-cognition, have been due to lack of curricular sophistication. Objectives related to such outcomes have not been adequately inherent in the experimental treatments.

These are clearly not mutually exclusive suggestions, nor do they represent a consistent point of view concerning the relationship between cognition, programming, applications software, and curriculum. But they do suggest that the results of research which may be seriously flawed, should not discourage those who have experienced the impact that the study of programming and computer application has had on students.

Even if it could be demonstrated that programming is a good option, it might not be the best option. Concurrent with the development of the computer as tutee, was the development of the computer as tutor. The potential of the computer as an instructional medium has become increasingly evident, more and more non-programming software is being prepared that addresses problem solving and simulations. Despite early concerns about the usefulness of microcomputers for anything beyond routine drill and practice, there are now available a good selection of computer assisted instructional programs that can challenge a student's problem-solving skills.

Programs are being prepared that address specific problem-solving skills. These programs can be very engaging, and they provide an intellectually rich environment that should be as stimulating as the challenge of programming. They often have the added advantage of requiring minimum training on the part of the teacher. The prognosis is good, but the research support for these applications is even less than that for programming.

A possible scenario attractive to those interested in the application of technology to education involves introducing students in the primary and intermediate grades to problem solving through the use of skill-specific and simulation software. These students will arrive at junior high or high school with certain specific problem-solving strategies well in hand, and they will then have the opportunity to improve the skills to the more general problems that can be posed in the programming environments of LOGO or BASIC or Pascal.

It should be noted that the research on programming and the transfer of problem-solving skills has focused almost exclusively on LOGO, and LOGO being taught to young students. Extrapolation of this research to high school students and a curriculum based on BASIC or Pascal needs to be done cautiously until there is supportive research evidence more closely tied to the proposed setting. The previous discussion has been provided to show some of the complexities that are involved in this type of research, and to suggest some of the models and/or mechanisms that might guide this research.

In addition to more precise and analytical approaches that will better define what is meant by problem solving, the researcher who plans to investigate the use of microcomputers to teach problem solving needs to examine the research on general problem solving. Problem solving has been a continuing area of research interest for years, and computer science teachers, as well as teachers in general, should be aware of it. An introduction to this material is presented by Dudley-Marling and Owston (1988). Their review summarizes the general research on problem solving and the claims that microcomputers can be used to teach generalized thinking and problem-solving skills.

Computer Literacy

At the present time at least 80% of all states recommend that students receive instruction in computers; eleven states have a computer literacy course requirement for high school graduation and five other states require students to pass a computer test or demonstrate competency (Electronic Learning 1987). This is very much in keeping with the consensus about what should be part of the required high school curriculum. In the 1985 Gallup poll, computer training was rated as fifth most important subject matter for high school graduates by a representative sample of the general public.

In some states, like Florida, competencies have been established across the curriculum, and students are expected to meet specific objectives at different points in the curriculum; competency checks are made at grades 3, 5, 8, and 11. Students must demonstrate specific competencies in order to be promoted and/or graduated.

Other states have approached the computer literacy issue by mandating that all students pass a required computer course. For example, the state of Texas (1986) has mandated a junior high school class in computer literacy. The course has well-defined objectives and guidelines for development.

Either approach, a list of competencies or a required course, leads to an operational definition of computer literacy. Certainly there are many acceptable ways to define computer literacy, but some may be better than others. Care must be taken not to define it in such a limited way as to make it trivial. The skills should lead to future, more sophisticated learning. An excellent analysis of the various approaches to the computer literacy curriculum has been prepared by Culbertson (1986); he suggests that various approaches to defining computer literacy can be classified into four categories (1) operational literacy; (2) instrumental literacy; (3) algorithmic reasoning; and (4) role-related literacy.

Operational Literacy. A curriculum which suggests that all the average student needs is some hands-on experience with a computer and some simple ideas about how a computer operates is categorized as being "operational literacy." The arguments for this approach are that it requires little resources, limited teacher training, and can be assimilated into the curriculum with minimum disruption for the ongoing program. But the approach is subject to the criticism that the information provided may be trivial, outdated, and might not lead to more advanced learning. Advocates of operational literacy for every student often recommend a more thorough or advanced level of literacy for those with special needs.

Instrumental Literacy. "Instrumental literacy" is based on the idea that students should learn to use the computer in the context of learning some other subject matter. The computer is viewed as an instructional tool to be used across the curriculum. This approach can focus on using some applications softwares such as a data base, or it might involve using some computer assisted instructional (CAI) package to teach or reinforce instructional content. Obviously this approach requires more resources and more training than operational literacy, but it can be assimilated into the curriculum in a constructive and positive manner. It may lead to more advanced learning or skills, but these skills and advanced knowledge are typically in the area in which the computer is used to augment, and not in the area of computer science or education. Critics of this approach raise the issues that the software that might be used can become obsolete very quickly, or in the case of CAI, the software may be less efficient than alternative instructional modes. Although ample research shows that CAI can be effective in drill and practice, its value or effectiveness at higher cognitive levels is still to be demonstrated.

Algorithmic Reasoning. Culbertson's third classification, "algorithmic reasoning," focuses on problem solving; the development of reasoning skills and insights into mathematical abstractions. Computer literacy advocates who argue for the teaching of programming support this level of literacy. The arguments are based on the propositional thinking required and the active role that the learner assumes in writing programs. As already discussed the research base for this approach is still rather meager, and controversial, but the potential benefits to the learner are at a higher level than the alternative curriculum. It is argued that programming leads to more generic skills, but even here Culbertson cautions that the generic skills may turn out to be too narrowly based to warrant the investment of time and resources.

Role-Related Literacy. The fourth computer literacy category is defined in terms of how computers are effecting the various roles that people assume in their day-to-day lives. In one role, the computer is viewed as an appliance, and ordinary citizens should know something about hardware and software in their role as consumers. From another point of view the computer is looked upon as a tool in the workplace, and the students should understand the computer as it pertains to specific tasks. Still a third role is that of the student in controlling the impact of computers on the quality of lives, particularly with respect to communication, politics and privacy. "Role-related literacy" places a host of responsibilities on the schools, not the least of which is determining the many roles that students might have with respect to the computer.

Culbertson's four categories of literacy are not mutually exclusive; many curriculum projects in computer education try to arrive at some blend of goals and objectives that stem from a multifaceted view of what the new technology offers. The categories can be useful when examining the rationale for a course or program in computer literacy because they suggest more generic characteristics or qualifications. As Culbertson noted, the computer is only a small figure in the overall electronic medium that is impacting all aspects of our lives. He suggests a broad concept of "telematic literacy" might better represent the view needed in an information society; a view which subsumes the smaller window of the computer as personal tool which opened with the advent of the microcomputer.

The argument might better be raised at this point for making a goal that is less specific than "computer literacy" or "telematic literacy." The focus of discussion could be expanded to one of technology literacy. As recommended by Boyer (1983), the high school curriculum needs to address the whole range of technological innovations that affect our society.

Individual teachers or curriculum committees may need to address the more immediate issue of whether programming is an essential curriculum component, or whether learning to use an applications package might be more appropriate, or the issue of whether placing a computer literacy course at the junior high level sufficiently addresses the needs of students in an information-age society. Educators and parents most be aware of the more complex issues of providing adequate technological training that is meaningful in the present and in the future.

CHOOSING A LANGUAGE

Earlier in this chapter, the history, options and status of the three dominant computer languages in the schools were presented. The debate over the choice of a language for teaching novices to program is intense. Every programmer has an opinion and is willing, if not anxious, to express it.

The issues are starting to be more broadly based with consideration being given to languages based on fundamentally different approaches to the computer-human interface (Hutchins 1986). BASIC, LOGO and Pascal, as well as most other programming languages, are based on a metaphor that the interface between man and computer should take place using a language in a conversational mode. This approach is healthy because it attempts to make the conversations more precise and at the same time closer to a more natural syntax and semantics. Voice input and natural language programming are direct responses to this conceptualization.

But the "conversational metaphor" is not the only option. An emerging alternative is what is called the "direct manipulation" metaphor in which the information contained within the computer is treated as if it were an object—a paper, a file, a picture, etc. Through icons, pointers, and tools, the images are manipulated on the screen as if they were objects. The desktop concept used on the Macintosh computer exemplifies this approach. The user is not require to know the specific language that is understood by the computer. Each image does, of course, have a physical counterpart, but the user does not need to understand its true nature to use the system.

At the present time, the direct manipulation concept is being used in a limited way to simplify the operating systems of some computers, most notably the Macintosh. The languages being taught remain those that have been established in the schools, but it is very clear that the direct manipulative approach to systems has had a significant effect on the ease of introducing students to programming. In the short run, the use of the desktop analogy will provide more time for teaching the logic and design of a program, because less time will be consumed teaching how to save a file and access a printer. In the long run, the teaching of object oriented languages like Smalltalk may work their way into the curriculum as alternatives. This is because as more and more applications software makes use of the direct manipulative interface, there will be more need to understand how it works.

Owen (1987) argues that direct manipulation and procedural reasoning are two very different skills that need to be examined as more complex interfaces are developed for computers. The arguments concerning which language is to be taught to the novice programmer may become more sophisticated in the next few years.

In addition to the arguments for consideration of the direct manipulation interface, there are those computer educators who suggest that novices are better served through introduction to a computer language which is logic-based or declarative. In a declarative language, the programmer's responsibility is to declare or clarify the problem through the description of facts or relationships which the computer can act upon, using the computational and inferential capabilities built into the language. In this environment there is less need to deal with iterations, data types, or algebraic expression, and more focus on the organization of knowledge, defining relationships and applying logic. Johanson (1988) has suggested that the work on Prolog, a new declarative language, makes it an alternative to the common introductory languages worthy of our consideration.

The question of the appropriate language for beginners is one that will not go away, but for the time being this discussion takes the more pragmatic view of the choices being limited to BASIC, LOGO and Pascal. Within this arena, the issues remain (1) what language to teach a novice programmer, and (2) where in the curriculum should the language be introduced? As one might expect, there is no consensus; however, the arguments for different implementations are becoming more refined and some data is starting to appear that might help narrow the choices.

LOGO

As discussed earlier, LOGO is one of the three languages most often considered for precollege students. The popularity of LOGO does not mean that it without its detractors. The most active controversy in educational computing has to do with the value or efficacy of LOGO as a programming language for novices. Teachers who were at the vanguard of computers in the schools started with a "quick and dirty" introduction to BASIC which was obviously not a language for the elementary grades, but it was the only game in town.

The advent of LOGO on the microcomputer, accompanied by the progressivist text by Papert (1980) brought about an enthusiastic and highly energetic movement for the teaching of programming as a core for the curriculum. The proposition was that LOGO was a computer language for the classroom that was based on research at the Massachuset Institute of Technology. The research utilized a Piagetian concept of child development, and it suggested that children could be taught to learn about learning. The research lead to the development of a legitimate programming language endorsed by eminent scientists and scholars. LOGO was hard to resist.

The value of LOGO is the most widely discussed topic in·the computer education literature. A study by Rubincam (1987) showed that Papert is cited twice as often as any other author in computer related articles. Educational journals are full of articles related to classroom experiences with LOGO or reviews of different versions of the LOGO language. Where there are research results, the value of LOGO as an instructional method remains in question because of conflicting conclusions.

The research is not conclusive; almost everyone would agree that the claims that have been made about the power of LOGO in the development of cognitive skills in young children in preschool and the primary grades is still not supported by research. Although there is substantial anecdotal evidence that children like to work with LOGO, and that they can learn to produce interesting pictures and patterns, evidence for the development of cognitive and prob-lem-solving skills remains in dispute.

The ambiguous research reports have caused Papert, and his followers, to become more defensive. In a recent article, Papert (1987) proposed that traditional research methods with control groups can not realistically be applied in the LOGO environment because LOGO requires a more holistic approach to education which is not amendable to analysis. He suggested instead an ap-proach based on literary and social criticism. Although the idea of software criticism has appeal due to the potential impact of com-puters on education and the schooling of children, it seemed that the development of such an approach might not be consistent with what we know about instruction and curriculum and schooling.

Papert has suggested that LOGO is being spoiled by the tech-nocentric thinking that surrounds the critical reviews and that this thinking tends to detract from the value and potential of the LOGO environment. His defense of LOGO did not go unanswered. Pea (1987) responded by calling to mind that Papert was one of those most responsible for the technocentric thinking in the first place, and not only was his presentation inconsistent, but it misrepre-sented the facts as related to the Bank Street School, where a fair amount of the critical research was done.

Another rejoinder by Walker (1987) was a little less severe, but nevertheless extremely critical of Papert's proposal that the LOGO community need not be subject to providing evidence of the long-term benefits of LOGO. He suggests that Papert take a more con-ciliatory approach to those who are interested in examining the merits of LOGO.

A third article, written in direct response to the Papert position paper on LOGO and research by Becker (1987), points out that over forty thousand teachers are using LOGO in their classrooms. But, for the most part, they are not using it as suggested by Papert. It is taught in learning environments that are not distinguishable from other computer-using environments, or in schools that are not noticeably different from other schools. Papert has suggested that if LOGO is to be effective, it has to be taught in an environment which is open, responsive, and unstructured. Teachers should be alerted to this fact. Many teachers are surprised to hear that LOGO is not designed for the traditional classroom.

Moursund's commentaries on LOGO, (1983–84, 1986) provide a balanced assessment of LOGO and its potential for the classroom teacher. Although he respects LOGO as a computer language, and advocates its use in the classroom, he concludes that proper utilization of LOGO requires (1) the availability of appropriate hardware and software, (2) an understanding on the part of the teacher of how to teach problem solving, and (3) a commitment by the teacher to discovery-based education and individualized instruction. From a pragmatic point of view, as desirable as providing the LOGO experience might be for children, these conditions will only be met in a small number of classrooms.

The problems with implementation of LOGO are really more substantive than people are sometimes led to believe. What started out as a panacea for the ailments of schools in general became an idea that the language could only be taught by experienced teachers capable of dealing in an open environment; this view was followed by suggestions that LOGO worked with different children in different ways. Now the promotion says that the power of LOGO can only be unleashed in a total school environment committed to free exploration and inquiry.

This is not to suggest that LOGO can have a negative effect on children's learning; there is no evidence to support this. The problem with LOGO may be that it is seriously flawed in conception in the very areas that the authors claim are its strengths. As an introductory computer language for the young child, LOGO lacks a sound psychological basis. Rather than assisting children to become more formal thinkers, the language may require students who are formal thinkers.

In order to use LOGO a student must be have the following skills:

1. He must be able to view the "Turtle" (usually a triangle) on the screen as an object which moves on the surface of the screen.
2. He must place himself in the position of turtle facing a particular direction on the screen.
3. He must not only know the concept of relative position, but he must be able to place himself in a relative coordinate system.

4. He must have a concept of scale in which numbers correspond to distances in one case and in another to angles of rotation.
5. He must view the screen as being a continuum which wraps around from top to bottom, bottom to top, right to left, and left to right.
6. He must deal with a keyboard which sometimes causes the turtle to move (immediate mode), other times prints letters (editing mode), and other times causes things to happen on the screen (run mode).
7. He must deal with a language which he has not spoken, nor has he heard spoken, which has a unique syntax and logic requiring an unusual sequence of words and phrases.

One need not work with young children to uncover the difficulties inherent in the popular LOGO implementations. Teachers learning the syntax of LOGO have a great deal of trouble trying to understand these very same things, and it is not because of the syntax. Learning to draw a box in LOGO is not a trivial activity, and learning to use procedures seems to be beyond many learners, students and teachers alike.

Of course, there are those who would argue that the child will learn these things as they work in the LOGO environment, but the overwhelming evidence from child development studies would say that these skills are not possible for the young child, and Piaget's research would say that it is impossible to teach this type of reasoning until the child has developed sufficiently. Of course, there are differences in opinion about the value of an experientially rich environment on cognitive development.

This is not to belittle the reports of high interest and constructive activity surrounding the use of LOGO in the primary and intermediate grades. Students are truly excited about their work, and there are numerous reports of student achievements. LOGO does provide entry to the cognitively rich environment of the computer, but there are no longitudinal studies to support the value of LOGO as a factor in effective use of this environment. Students in general cannot and do not work with LOGO in the manner its writers have suggested. Becker's data (1987) shows that although forty thousand teachers are using LOGO in their classes, nearly three quarters of them use it for enrichment rather than regular instruction.

To understand the LOGO phenomenon, one needs to be aware that the research laboratory which produced LOGO was just that, a research lab, not a typical classroom. One of the earliest projects using LOGO was done in Lexington, Massachusetts with twelve seventh grade students in a program designed to teach mathematics (Feurzeig et al. 1969). The students used teletype machines linked to a mainframe computer through an acoustic coupler; the LOGO version had no graphic capabilities, and the intent was not so much to see how students think, or how they thought about their thinking; rather, a curriculum was being developed to make mathematics more understandable.

Although the projected audience for the language was the classroom, the developmental settings were far from typical, as has been the case with most curriculum reforms. The novelty of the approach and the expense of the equipment in the late sixties and seventies may have precluded widespread field testing, but today's advocates often do not acknowledge the limited field testing that has been done.

The only study that can be found of LOGO being taught in a "realistic school setting" (Massachusetts Institute of Technology 1977, 4) was in the Brookline school district in 1977/78, in which there were four microcomputers, a "turtle" tethered to the computer, and classes of four students working with a single teacher and under frequent observation by staff along with outside evaluators (Papert et al 1979). The actual study involved only sixteen sixth grade students.

It was not that the researchers didn't understand the problem of "ivory tower" research losing something in the transition to the schools; their own proposals (Massachusetts Institute of Technology 1977, 8–11) acknowledged how they intended to deal with the problem, but the issues were overlooked when the language took on commercial possibilities, and were presented to the education community as an answer to how computers might reach their potential in schools. The research base was limited to a small number of students in atypical settings. As stated earlier, the most recent response to this process has been that typical research approaches are not appropriate for a program as comprehensive as LOGO, but that a new, more holistic approach is required to assess its impact (Papert 1987). The debate is interesting and ongoing; it may certainly help define the role of computers in the schools.

The computer science teacher should be aware of the controversy, and its background. The subjects in the early studies were not young primary age students, but more often the students were in an intermediate grade level or higher; they could have been at the level of formal thought. More importantly, the students did not deal with the abstraction of a triangle moving across the surface of a screen, but rather they worked with an actual robot that was tethered to a computer. The "turtle" was real, and they watched it move and they watched the pen go up and down, so they could imagine themselves riding on the turtle's back when they directed it to move right or left. The language is abstract, but the instruction was object oriented. Something crucial might have been lost in the adaptation of LOGO to the microcomputer, which by necessity uses abstract or symbolic representations.

The research on LOGO has been exploratory and developmental rather than experimental and comprehensive. But the interest persists, and even though the questions raised in the controversy may be frustrating to people who expect more from educational research, the questions may lead to a greater impact on education than the original expectations.

As noted earlier, it is surprising that LOGO is recommended for use as early as kindergarten or that some states have accepted it as the recommended language for young children.

The problem with the unquestioning support that is sometimes given to a language like LOGO is that it can raise expectations which are not going to be fulfilled in the short term, and the credibility of programming as a viable subject for the school may be diminished. This is not to say that LOGO should not be used in the elementary or high school; the expectations, however, must be more reasonable. More research is necessary on LOGO in terms of practical problems and where the difficulties can be anticipated. Cohen's detailed accounting of a seven-month study in a classroom (1987) provides valuable information for teachers about student learning of LOGO compared to other studies that try to test how LOGO instruction affects other academic skills and attitudes.

On the positive side, it should be noted that LOGO is a language that was devised from LISP, and much of the professional support for the language comes from those who realize that instruction in LOGO, if done at an appropriate level, could lay a strong foundation for learning other procedural languages such as LISP or Pascal. Most implementations of LOGO are very powerful languages which have the capacity for rigorous applications of character and string manipulation, but most teachers cannot get beyond the turtle graphics. Someone may remove the turtle graphics from LOGO and market it as LISP for the microcomputer. Not only would it have greater academic respectability, but it would provide another option for the serious high school programming class. A modest attempt to do this was reported in a study by Kurland, Pea, Clement and Mawby (1986). A group of experienced high school programming students were provided nine weeks of instruction on each of three different languages. The LOGO segment was done solely with list processing and no turtle graphics.

LOGO versus BASIC

A critical commentary on LOGO as a language should not be interpreted as an argument for teaching BASIC to the novice programmer. If LOGO is ruled out as an introductory language, then the same criteria must be applied to BASIC. The problems are very similar, and in the case of BASIC there is even less research on its effectiveness with students. But no one has suggested that BASIC as a cure-all for the schools. Typically BASIC is not viewed as appropriate below the third grade because the standard versions require the use of line numbers and most have relatively "unfriendly" editors. As versions with better editors become available, this situation may improve.

In the high school, BASIC has been taught as a computational language, and it required a confusing array of skills and knowledge that were foreign to many teachers. Nevertheless, the engaging power of the computer with young children and adolescents cannot be overlooked. Children are fascinated with programming; teachers are challenged with teaching the subject.

Comparative studies of BASIC versus LOGO seem to be nonexistent. The initial disillusionment with BASIC and the enthusiasm for LOGO, has led to an almost complete loss of interest in BASIC in the elementary schools. But some teachers are finding that the introduction of BASIC through graphics can be very engaging, tapping the same creative elements that make turtle graphics so attractive to the young programmer. BASIC has the advantage that it usually is an interpreted language, and the speed of access has advantages over a compiled language. If a student's introduction to a programming language is limited to graphics, then low-resolution BASIC may be as good as, if not better than, LOGO.

BASIC versus Pascal

The comparisons of BASIC and Pascal can be made on two different, but practical levels. There are technical differences between the two languages which lead to significant differences in their ability to solve certain types of problems. There are practical differences in the two languages which impact their present and future use in the schools.

Technical Differences. The differences between BASIC and Pascal are not merely syntactical, the languages are fundamentally different in the way they organize programs and data. One of the most significant differences is the ability of Pascal to use a variety of data types; whereas BASIC is typically limited to three data types—floating point, integer, and alphanumeric. Not only can a variable be defined as to type in Pascal, but the range of values can also be limited to a subrange.

Since the user defines both variable types and subrange of values in Pascal, the program need not include extensive checking of variables for type and value. This allows concise expressions of code, which are tedious, if not impossible, to duplicate in BASIC.

BASIC is typically an interpreted language on a microcomputer, and because of the line-by-line processing of code, there are minimal requirements governing program structure or context. Aside from dimensioning of arrays, most versions of BASIC are only controlled by checking the syntax of the line that is being interpreted, and then only when the program is actually running.

Pascal, on the other hand, requires that the program be developed through a series of blocks; each block must have two segments, one which defines variables, variable types, and other data definitions, the other containing the logic or algorithm that performs the function or action of the block. Each block or module is essentially an independent unit. Pascal is typically a compiled language, and during the compiling of the modules, the modules are checked for syntax errors as well as consistency in the use of data types and structures.

Pascal also has a number of algorithm expressions that facilitate programming, which are not available in BASIC. Some examples are logical operators ("and," "or," and "not"), conditional statements ("If . . . then . . . else" and "case") and repetitive statements ("Repeat . . . until" and "Do . . . while"). These features not only make programming easier, but add to the clarity of the code making it more concise and precise.

As mentioned earlier, the data definitions of Pascal extend the simple data types to include: a defined scalar type, which limits the values a scalar can have by providing a list, and a Boolean type which is extremely useful for program control functions depending on true or false conditions. In addition, Pascal provides structured types—arrays, records, sets, files, and pointers—which can be manipulated in much the same ways as simple variables. For those interested in an introduction to these concepts, an article by Mundie (1978) is recommended.

The point here is that these structures provide ways of organizing and manipulating data that would be very difficult to do in BASIC. It should be kept in mind that some of these differences would not be significant in an introductory course, because concepts like files and pointers are not covered. Also, BASIC is a programming language that continues to evolve, and the differences between some of the more recent versions of BASIC and Pascal are not as numerous as the preceding discussion might indicate.

Practical Considerations. The pragmatic curriculum differences between BASIC and Pascal point to the wide acceptance of BASIC as the principle programming language at the high school level. The argument over whether or not BASIC is an acceptable introductory language is almost moot. The national assessment of computer literacy (Martinez and Mead 1988) showed that although 91.9% of computer coordinators indicated that they knew BASIC, only 35.4% knew LOGO and 35.5% Pascal. Unless there is a major change in the preparation of teachers, Pascal will not become the dominant instructional language at the high school level.

Not only are there few teachers prepared to teach Pascal, but the economics of selecting another language over BASIC makes it almost prohibitive. BASIC remains the resident language in most computers used in the K-12 environment. As noted earlier in this chapter, several adaptations of BASIC are available (see Appendix C) which can offset the criticisms of the kind of "street" BASIC which has been so common in the schools.

RECOMMENDED READING

Seymour Papert *Mindstorms: Children, Computers and Powerful Ideas.* Basic Books, 1980. The book that lit the fire which brought all the attention to LOGO. Needs to be read to understand the enthusiasm that some have for LOGO.

David D. Thornburg, "A Computer Language at the Crossroads." *A + Magazine*, Vol. 4, No. 3, March 1986, pp. 78–84. A frank discussion of the difficulties LOGO has had in being accepted as a real programming language as compared to a language for teaching children to draw boxes. It explores the real value of having a procedural language with all the graphic capabilities of LOGO as a tool in a very rich, creative environment.

"A Dynamic Decade of Development," *Understanding Computers: Computer Languages*, Time-Life Books, Alexandria, Virginia, 1986, pp. 67–98

"Programming Comes Home," *Understanding Computers: Computer Languages*, Time-Life Books, Alexandria, Virginia, 1986, pp. 99–121. Excellent narratives on the historical events in the development of languages for the microcomputer starting with Tiny BASIC through LOGO.

John G. Kemeny and Thomas E. Kurtz, *Back to BASIC: The History, Corruption and Future of the Language*. Addison-Wesley Publishing Company, Inc., Reading Massachusetts, 1985. The notion that programming should be a common or universal skill had its origins in the work at Dartmouth in the mid-sixties. This accounting of the activities and philosophy behind the work should lead to a better understanding of the current issues surrounding the role of BASIC in the schools.

SUGGESTED ACTIVITIES

1. Prepare a program that will ask a student his/her name and then print out the name on a blank screen. Prepare the program in BASIC, LOGO, and Pascal.

2. Scan the issues of one of the weekly computer magazines— *Infoworld, MacWEEK, PC WEEK*—and obtain a copy of an article which describes an application of BASIC programming in a current situation and/or a review of a current modification or adaptation of BASIC. Prepare a paper which decribes the implications of the article for the classroom teacher. If there are no implications, make a clear statement as to why.

3. Scan the current issues of *The Computing Teacher, Classroom Computing News* and/or *Electronic Learning* and locate an article on the use of LOGO. Respond to the implications of the application for a high school teacher who was teaching programming in a school district where another teacher implemented the proposed program.

CHAPTER 5
INSTRUCTIONAL METHODS AND STRATEGIES

INTRODUCTION

Teaching structured programming may lead to greater problem-solving skills, but only if the instruction is done within the context of a well-presented and organized course. Experienced teachers understand the requirements of the classroom which establish the context for instruction, but the novice instructor might profit from viewing the application of generic methods to the teaching of programming. This chapter is for the beginning teacher; it suggests methods that might be useful in setting an atmosphere for the teaching of structured programming.

Methods are the activities and strategies used in the classroom to accomplish the stated objectives. A teacher needs to have a variety of activities and strategies in order to meet the many needs students have. Ideally, informed research will be available to indicate which methods are more effective than others.

The purpose of this chapter is to provide a guide to various procedures and strategies, and, when possible, to point to the research findings or the authoritative experience supporting a particular approach that facilitates classroom learning. It is well known that many teachers model the behavior of the teacher that they worked with in student teaching. When a good model is available, this can be an excellent introduction to the profession. In the case of computer science, however, there are a very limited number of teachers available that have extensive preparation and/or experience, so a beginning teacher might not get the best role model. In any case, a teacher should be alert and selective in the incorporation of strategies and procedures into an instructional repertoire.

Teaching is still an art, not a science. Certainly we do not know enough about learning in general, and even less about the process of learning computer skills, to be able to prescribe instruction. A teacher should develop a style that reflects his or her personality and values. Hopefully within the individual teacher's personality and values are those intellectual and creative instincts that will make the classroom a special place for students, a special place for learning.

The basic axiom for selection of teaching methods is: *"methods are selected on the basis of the objective to be achieved"*. A method is not selected merely because it is novel or fun; it must be consistent with the objective of the lesson or unit. The corollary of this is that the objectives are selected on the basis of the goals, and this is where we need to begin when we are planning instruction.

GOALS

Although there is considerable controversy about what is meant by "computer literacy", there is almost no argument against the idea that all students graduating from our schools need to be computer literate. The goal is clear; the objectives are still a matter of debate. It is not our purpose to present the pros and cons of this debate, but merely to make it clear that the issues are not resolved, and that the use of the term "computer literacy" does not necessarily add to the clarity of a discussion or a debate.

At the risk of entering into the controversy, it is suggested that most informed computer science teachers would agree that every student should meet the following performance objectives in order to be considered computer literate:

1. Recognize that the computer is a tool that can be used to solve both simple and complex problems.
2. Know that a computer is made up of various functional components.
3. Be able to develop at least a minimal program in a higher level language.
4. Be able to use at least one applications program.

Many students meet these objectives before they get the option of selecting a high school computer science class. Students electing a high school class in computer science have a wide range of differing goals; this makes curriculum planning difficult.

The objectives for a high school computer science course need to be varied because a high school course can be used by students with different goals and objectives in mind. Some students will be interested in computer science because they envision a career as a programmer or electrical engineer, and they need as much experience and background as they can get out of high school. There will be others in a typical class who will be looking for the academic challenge that a computer science course can provide, but are not necessarily looking at it as leading to a career. There is third group who will be taking the course because they have been told that it is an essential component of any career that they might be interested in in the future. Hopefully, there will be a fourth group who are taking the course because they heard it was a good course with a good teacher.

The goals for these four groups are not the same; consequently the objectives will not be the same. If this is the case, an effort must be made to organize the instruction to meet as many goals as possible. This is a challenging task for even the most experienced teacher.

Part of resolving the problem is deciding what components of a course might meet the needs different kinds of students have in common. According to the Task Force on Curriculum for Secondary School Computer Science (1985), an introductory computer science course would have the following objectives:

1. The student should learn general problem-solving techniques and be able to:

   clearly define problems,
   subdivide problems into logical modules,
   design structured solutions to problems (algorithms),
   code algorithms into a specific language,
   hand trace algorithms and code, and
   test and debug programs.

2. The student should understand the uses and limitations of a high-level language with regards to:

   the available data structures and
   the available control structures.

3. The student should be able to implement solutions in a specific high-level language for the major types of programming problems.
4. The student should be able to anticipate, identify, isolate, and correct errors.

The Association for Computing Machinery committee recommends a two course sequence, or a year of computer science; the second half of the course is an extension of the first half with some attention being given to applications software and hardware.

These are a reasonable set of planning objectives for all four groups of students. The more specific objectives might be written to provide for some flexibility among students, or a course might be designed in such a way that the students select objectives they would like to be evaluated on in order to prove their competency. More about the latter when course organization and student evaluation are described.

Again, the task for a teacher is to develop a course which takes into account the range of goals and objectives that their students might have or need. Some guidelines are available and some planning objectives have been articulated, but these are only starting points for developing a curriculum.

INSTRUCTIONAL ORGANIZATION

The process for planning instruction is straightforward. A course is divided into units, units are divided into lessons, and lessons are divided into activities. This approach should be comfortable for those familiar with the hierarchial structure of programming. The course might be viewed as the main module which establishes the flow of control in the course, and within this module the goals for the entire program would be expressed. The top level of the hierarchy would be the units, each with its specific objectives. At level 2 and beyond, each module would perform one or more specific activities.

Units

Each unit has a focus or theme which provides a guide or sets the criteria for selection of content. A unit might be defined in terms of the period of time, possibly as short as two weeks, and maybe extending for six to eight weeks. A beginning computer course might have the following units:

Unit 1: Problem Solving and Top-Down Design (2 weeks)
Unit 2: Development of Modules (2 weeks)
Unit 3: Writing Code (4 weeks)
Unit 4: Computer Components (2 weeks)
Unit 5: Applications Software (3 weeks)
Unit 6: Social Issues (2 weeks)

The six units would make up the course. Each unit would be self-contained, but they might overlap. During the time periods of the latter units, certain activities begun in earlier units could be continued or completed. It is very important that a teacher plan how he will distribute the time he has for teaching a course. There is always more information available on any topic or unit than can possibly be taught in the time period provided. Without a master plan to work from, a teacher could spend all his time on a single topic, and deny his students the full scope of the course. In some cases, where a course is a prerequisite to another course, or where an external examination is required, failure to cover the stipulated syllabus might be very harmful to the students.

A beginning teacher will find it hard to estimate the time required to teach a topic, but unless there is a schedule and discipline, one can lose track of goals and objectives.

The following might represent a unit plan for Unit 1 above:

TITLE: Introduction to Computers and Problem Solving

GOAL: To understand that a computer is a tool that is used for problem solving.

OBJECTIVES: By the end of this unit, each student will:

1. Demonstrate the proper technique of inserting a disk, turning on the computer, and running a program. Each student will be required to do this at some time after the first laboratory session when asked to do so by the instructor or a laboratory assistant. A checklist of names will be

used to be sure that each student has done so.

2. Demonstrate his knowledge of the five functional parts of the computer and their relationships to each other by correctly labeling and drawing control lines on a diagram provided on the unit test.

3. Demonstrate his ability to use the six commands associated with low resolution graphics by including each of them in the program written as part of laboratory exercise #1.

4. Prepare a list of not less than five different uses of computers when asked to do so on a unit test.

5. Define correctly at least five of the following terms on the unit test—RAM, ROM, "spaghetti code," syntax error, input, output, memory.

6. Explain in his own language on the unit test how each of the following terms is used in relationship to computers—specification, sequence, context, module.

7. Given a set of activities related to the planning of a party, prepare a structure chart.

TIME: 2 Weeks (5 lectures, 4 laboratory sessions, 1 test period)

PREREQUISITES: None

TOPICS: 1. The Computer as Tool
    a. "number crunching"
    b. simulations
    c. word processing
    d. communications
    2. The Ubiquitous Computer
    a. definition
    b. functional parts
    3. Problem Solving

a. specification
b. planning
c. outlining
d. part-whole relationships
4. Top-Down Design
5. Characteristics of Program
  A. syntax
  B. sequence
  C. context

VOCABULARY: All terms in topic outline plus input, output, CPU, memory, storage, disk, "K", RAM, ROM, microprocessor, boot, run, syntax error, "spaghetti code," module, line number, structure chart.

COMMANDS: GR, PLOT, COLOR, HLIN, VLIN, REM, END.

PROGRAMMING ASSIGNMENT: Lab #1—The preparation of a low resolution graphic which includes the use of at least three colors, and all the commands presented in the unit above.

HOMEWORK ASSIGNMENTS: Prepare a list of the things you own that contain a microprocessor.

EXTRA CREDIT: Prepare a paper of between 300–500 words on someone who has made a significant contribution to computer science who lived prior to 1950. Sign up for names on list posted. No student can use a person already taken.

FILMS: From Pebbles to Programs—Part 1 (30 minutes)

SOFTWARE: Student Sample Disk I

HANDOUTS: Lab Number I
Command List I
Extra Credit Assignment I
Low Resolution Screen Template

Vocabulary List I
Functional Part Diagram

FORMATIVE Terminology Crossword Puzzle
EVALUATION: Low Resolution Debugging Exercise
Function Model Diagram
Film Checklist—From Pebbles to Programs—Part 1

TRANSPARENCIES: Topic Outlines #1 & #2
Definition of Computer
Functional Model of Computer
Top-Down Design #1, #2, #3, & #4

EVALUATION: Lab Experiment I   100 points
Unit Test   100 points
Assignment   25 points
Film Checklist   10 points
Extra Credit   50 points

The unit plan above gives a sense of what the teacher intends to during the first two weeks of the course. Obviously a large number of decisions have been made, and plans have been developed to the point that two people using the plan would probably provide very similar instruction.

One thing that is known about learning is that it is a structured process, and that the structure most come from somewhere. Some students can develop their own structure, or build the new information into existing schemas, but for the most part, it is the instructor's responsibility to make the structure apparent, and to make the linkages with prior learning clear and explicit. The unit plan forces the instructor to commit himself to an overall structure.

It can also be seen that the instructor has planned to get the students working on the computer during the first two weeks, and that he is using low resolution graphics rather than print statements as his introduction to syntax and programming.

Almost as important as what is in the plan is what has been excluded. It might be noted that, except for the extra credit assignment, there is no mention of the history of computers. It might also be noted that there is no mention of bytes or bits or binary code. These things might come later in the course but they are not part of this introductory unit. Only the topics and terminology in the unit plan, or previous unit plans if there had been any, should be used, and if student raise questions about terms or ideas that are not in the plan, they should be played down or put off until they fit into the general plan. How far a teacher allows student questions to lead the course away from the plans that have been established is a question of judgment and style, but a teacher must always consider that a response to one student's curiosity can lead to many students' confusion.

Lessons

The understanding of the relationships between activities, objectives, and goals can be thought of as analogous to a structured chart in which the level 0 module is the goal for the unit and the lesson modules represent the various level 1 modules. Each lesson performs a single function which is designed to accomplish a single objective. (Although it is not necessary, it is a good idea to think of a lesson as the amount of instruction that might be provided in a single day even though sometimes lessons extend over several days.)

Engagement. Each lesson has an introduction. The purpose of the introduction is to get the attention of the students away from what they have been thinking about, and to start them thinking about what the instructor wants them to think about.

Some teachers merely start to talk, but this may not be effective in some classrooms. Computer science teachers are fortunate in that they do have a variety of visual devices to get the students' attention. For example, in the lesson that was described above, the instructor might start the first lesson by booting a demonstration program that shows a previous student assignment dealing with low resolution graphics. Not only can it be used to get attention, but the program demonstrates the expectation for the assignment.

Once a teacher has the students' attention, the trick is to glide into the actual content with as smooth a transition as possible. Possible strategies for the lessons are presented in the next section.

Exposition. Once the students are engaged, the subject matter is presented. This is the easy part of the lesson, if the instructor knows his subject matter. Because much of the professional preparation of a teacher is concerned with learning the content of the discipline, this should not be a problem.

There are, of course, differences in the way instructors teach the same content. Some teachers have a better appreciation of the logic and flow of the information, but more importantly they have a better understanding of the prior knowledge and values of their students. As Ausubel has suggested:

> If I had to reduce all of educational psychology to just one principle, I would say this: The most important single factor influencing learning is what the learner already knows. Ascertain this and teach him accordingly. (Ausubel et al. 1978, iv)

The actual information presented to students in a typical class may be very limited and require only a small portion of the actual lecture time. A good lecturer keeps in mind that the information needs to be placed in a meaningful context.

Elaboration. After the actual presentation of content, the next step is to see to it that the subject matter is learned. Learning is an active process. How does a teacher involve students in an active way during lessons? The activity does not have to be physical, but it needs to engage the student so that the new information will be somehow linked or anchored to the old. Ausubel et al. (1978, 5) say that in order to get meaningful learning, as opposed to rote memorization, a student needs to associate the new information with aspects of the individual's existing cognitive structure. The process of linking is known as elaboration.

One approach to elaboration is to have student verbalize what they are learning. Gagne and Smith (1962) showed that by having students verbalize each step in solving a problem, they become more efficient on future problems. In another study, Wittrock (1974) had students generate a one-sentence response to each paragraph they read, and their recall at the end of the exercise was nearly twice that of the control group.

Mayer (1980) performed an experiment in which students read a technical manual. The subjects in treatment group were directed to describe the new statements in terms of a concrete model of the computer. Although the control and treatment groups did not perform any differently on recall questions, those students who used the elaboration were superior in their response to problem-solving questions.

In a related experiment, students were asked to compare two related statements after reading a segment of text. The comparison-elaboration group excelled at problem-solving questions; both groups did about the same on retention questions.

In a third experiment, three groups were used: a control group, a model elaboration group, and a comparative elaboration group. The subjects were asked to recall portions of the text. Their responses were analyzed to see whether they were more conceptual or technical. Again the elaboration group showed a greater tendency to recall conceptual information.

What all these studies as well as many others point to, is that when the learner is actively involved, he is more likely to learn information that relates to higher order thinking.

Evaluation. It would be nice if one could assume that because their instruction was so well organized, the presentation so clear, and methods of elaboration so well designed, the students learned everything taught. This may happen, but we do need to get some sense of what is really being learned. It is best to do this on an on-going basis, rather than waiting until the unit is over and it is too late to remediate.

The concept of evaluating the effectiveness of instruction on an ongoing basis is known as formative evaluation. As often as can be done, a teacher should attempt to get a sense of the students' understanding of what is being taught. This can be done through their work on activities, responses to questions, or any number of overt activities. In the unit plan shown above, the instructor planned to assess student understandings through the use of crossword puzzles, practice quizzes, sample problem sets, and an examination. Each lesson has at least one formative evaluation activity, as well as the usual opportunities for questions and answers that arise during a lecture or instruction sequences.

Formative evaluation can be used as part of the grading process in a class, but some would prefer not to increase the pressure for grades included in the ongoing classroom activities. The best model is to think of formative evaluation as an assessment of the effectiveness of the instruction which can be used by the instructor to modify his/her teaching to insure learning. If the majority of students do not accomplish the intended level of performance as determined by a formative evaluation, the instructor can change the instructional program. Frequently, the performance objective provides the basis for the formative evaluation.

Empowering. It is not enough that a student learn something; he has to appreciate the fact that he has learned something. A lesson is not complete until the student feels that he has learned something, not merely responded correctly to a test item or performed some activity. To be empowered with new knowledge or skill, a student must have a sense of mastery.

Genuine praise for a job well done or satisfactory completion of a sample or practice exercise can help assure students that they have mastered the content of a lesson or unit.

Exit. In the final phase of any class, which in most cases is also the end of a lesson, a teacher needs to draw things together. This final activity on the part of the instructor is critical because it provides him/her with an opportunity to once again draw the students' attention to major concepts, to point out the logical structure of the material, and finally to set up the next class or laboratory period to follow. Not only is transition from lesson to lesson important as an organizational technique, but it can be a strong motivator.

The motivation can come from the fact that the closure portion of a lesson can make it clear to the students that they have learned what was being taught, or at least understood what was significant in the lesson. Closure also provides another opportunity to relate the content of the lesson to some relevant aspect of the students' present or future life.

Assignments

In a computer science class there are typically two types of assignments: those involving the instructional material (homework) and those related to the writing of programs (laboratory).

Homework. A teacher is sometimes surprised to find out that homework has not proven to have a significant effect on student achievement. (Richards 1982) This may have been due to the quality of the research, but the fact remains, homework of itself may not be an effective instructional strategy. Just as in the case of lecturing, homework which is not directed towards specific ends, and homework which does not include feedback, is likely to be unproductive. Homework tends to be dull, repetitious drill and practice, but it need not be that way.

Assignments can be very useful at providing students with the opportunity to be creative and to pursue individual goals and achievements. Homework assignments are the easiest part of the curriculum to individualize. For example, an assignment might be to explain a rule or a theory. This might be a very boring and uninteresting assignment, but it can be put into a creative mode. The student might be asked to explain a theory, but to do it using something other than a standard mode of communication. In response to such an assignment, theories have been presented as: (1) short plays with famous characters explaining their understanding of the theory; (2) a football cheer for the latest discovery; (3) a comic strip character explaining the concept to a child; (4) a limerick that might be used as a commercial; and other creative expressions.

The key here is that the assignment might not be required, and the mode of response not specified; in fact, specification can be kept to a minimum to avoid inhibiting the students.

Placing too much emphasis on homework as a part of a student's grade in a course can have counterproductive results. Work done outside of class, obviously, can be done with assistance that may lead to the work being of a quality that does not represent the student's knowledge of the subject or even his/her effort in producing the material.

Laboratory. Although programming assignments can lead to creative work as in the case of homework, there is a tendency to provide more of a focus in the assignment of laboratory exercises. Typically, the beginning series of exercises tend to be very predictable assignments leading to students becoming aware of how a computer is programmed with little interest in the actual programming task. It is not unusual for the first assignments to be mere copying of code into the computer with no consideration for actual program development.

Again, looking at the unit suggested above, the first programming assignment is an invitation to have the students create a graphic. The response is certainly not limited to a few lines of code. Within the first assignment, the seeds for structured programming, documentation, and problem solving are planted. The program quickly becomes a set of modules corresponding to the different features of the graphic, the code requires the inclusion of REM statements to separate the segments into distinct segments, and the thought of having something move on the screen is almost irresistible.

A computer programming course developed by Karl Jahns (1985) which focuses on structured programming rather than learning syntax has the following options for programming assignments in its first unit:

1. Make the letter "I" in the following way:

```
IIIIIII
  III
  III
  III
  III
IIIIIII
```

2. Find and display the circumference and the area of a circle after having been given the radius. Formulas are not necessary.
3. Write a program that will utilize the computer as launch control center for a rocket. Include countdown, launch and tracking.
4. After two numbers have been entered, print all of the even numbers between the two.
5. Ask for the user's name and age. If the age is less than 16 then print the message, "You're too young to drive."
6. Read 10 names from a data file. If the name begins with a letter between J and R, print the name in the middle of a box made of # symbols.
7. You've just had a birthday party where 12 people brought gifts. Create a program that will accept a name and a gift and print a "thank you" form letter.
8. Create a graphic picture of a house.
9. Develop a program to play the card game War. The computer deals 26 cards to two players. The top cards from each set are then compared. The highest card wins and both cards are placed in the bottom of that player's set of cards. Whoever runs out of cards first loses.
10. Make a program that simulates a bank machine. A code number will be asked for. If it matches a preset code then the user may withdraw the amount of cash entered next. The account will then be reduced by that amount. The account only has $150 to begin and it may not fall below $0.

In this approach, the student is not asked to actually produce the code that will lead to an operational program, but rather he constructs the pseudocode outline which can be translated into a set of dummy modules which would simulate the program. It is not clear from Jahns' presentation how many of the exercises are required, if any, but it certainly provides an interesting list of options for naive students to chose from.

As a programmer, a teacher could take almost any of the choices and very quickly start to imagine the particular programming segments that might be required. For example #8, a teacher might think that what is needed are walls, a roof, windows, doors, a chimney, a lawn, etc. Each item could be a separate module which would perform a specific function. Knowing nothing about the syntax of BASIC, but having been introduced to the idea of modules, top-down design, and rudimentary pseudocode, a student can move very quickly into a rich, creative, problem-solving environment. This course does demonstrate that it is possible to teach programming concepts before becoming involved in the syntax of a language.

Certainly the list of programming assignments is more than any one student might attempt during a two week unit. Possibly one assignment might be required and another be optional. The required assignment could be the same for all students, or both could be student choices. The more real student choice in the curriculum, the better. If assignments are going to be used to develop problem-solving skills and if the assignments are to challenge the potential of students, then the student must be active in both the development of the assignment and in its implementation. Giving students real choices does not necessarily lead to their making poor choices. In one of my classes there was an optional assignment which allowed a student to read a book on a selected topic that had been assigned for the quarter, and make a short report on the book. Up to four books could be read by a student each quarter, and the total proportion of their grade that might be gained by reading and reporting was ten percent. I had a student who was interested in being a journalist read four books each quarter—twelve books in total—for 100 out of 1000 points per quarter. In most high school situations, a teacher would find it very difficult to assign a student the task of reading a single book as part of a class assignment.

Evaluation

No matter what the student activity might be, the student needs to receive some affirmation or assessment to validate his effort. The form and extent of the evaluation will certainly be a matter of style and available resources, hopefully not limited to a report card grade. For our purposes, evaluation will be examined at three levels: feedback, assessment and grades.

Feedback. Feedback is information that is provided to a student relative to correctness, quality, or appropriateness of his/her response to a question or an assignment. At the lowest level, feedback is merely an indication whether the student is correct. This type of response is of little value when a student is not correct, but it does tend to affirm valid information. This is the type of response that a student gets from an editor in response to a syntax error.

At the second level of feedback, a student is provided with the correct answer when his response is not correct. Strangely enough, this is not always done; teachers often are too busy to provide this much information.

At the third level, a student is provided not only information about his response, but when necessary he receives corrective information. If remediation is necessary, then this form of feedback is necessary. Research has shown that when students receive feedback that does not include remediation, it has little effect on their learning. Bumgardner's research on the effectiveness of drill and practice on student's learning of mathematics facts (1984) has shown this to be true for CAI.

Assessment. When a teacher is dealing with determining whether a student has met an objective, the task is somewhat different. The criteria should be made explicit in the objectives, and all the person doing the assessment need do is to check the performance against the criteria. In the classroom this might be managed by the use of a checklist of objectives and criteria.

Assessment is different from feedback in that when a student fails to meet the objective, the instructor has to make a decision regarding whether the instruction should be repeated, or modified and tried again. Typically this involves some feedback to the student, but primarily it provides feedback to the instructor regarding the effectiveness of instruction.

In both cases, feedback and assessment, the criteria need to be objective, and the goal is to effect the instructional program. Grading is a completely different process.

Grading. Typically, grading is a process by which students are compared to other students. At times people tend to consider grades as an objective measure of the amount or quality of the performance, but its subjective aspects are easy to confirm. Certainly no one would argue that the assignment of a grade of "90" means that a student knows 90% of the material that was taught, let alone 90% of the total subject matter in a course. At best, a 90 indicates that a student's performance is better than those students with grades of 85 but not as good as those with 95.

Letter grades are easier to justify because they are by their very nature a measure of relative rank or position, but there is always the tendency to try to equate letter grades to percentages, for instance, an A is equal to 93%.

If a teacher can accept the fact that most grades are relative rather than absolute measures, they can use them to advantage in the teaching process. Students want to receive good grades. If a teacher can assure students that they will not in fact be judged according to their relative rank nor their relative knowledge of the subject matter, they may unleash a powerful desire to perform.

One such process is to assign each activity, test, and assignment some absolute point value. Students can then earn their grades by earning as many points as is necessary. They have certain optional activities and other required activities, but in the overall picture they design their own course of study within the framework set by the instructor. An example of such a system might be as follows:

Activity	Maximum Points	Number of Opportunities	Total Points
Quizzes*	50	5	250
Unit Test*	100	3	300
Laboratory Assignments*	25–100	10	500
Homework	10	10	100
Book Reports	25	4	100
Term Paper	100	1	100
Extra Credit Projects	25–50	4	150
Student Design Project	100	1	100

*Required activities

In this system, a student is required to take certain tests and participate in some laboratory work, but his performance in these areas can be augmented by other activities over which he has more control. There is even the option for the student to suggest an activity that might be added to his program.

Grades are assigned on the basis of total points with an A being assigned to 930 points, a B to 870 points, etc. If grades are assigned with a number, the grades can be converted directly; 990 points gives a grade of 99, 900 points results in a grade of 90, etc.

Students have a considerable amount of flexibility in such a program. In practice, with classes as large as one hundred and fifty students, students have been able to design programs in keeping with their own objectives. Although there is a tendency for students to focus on the more traditional pattern of quizzes and assignments to determine their grades, some students take the opportunity to extend themselves. A system like this works better with larger classes because the instructor has the opportunity to develop a large number of activities without committing himself to spending a large amount of time developing something that few, if any, students do. The only problem that has developed from this system is that a large number of students can, and do, earn high grades; sometimes administrators become concerned when the majority of students in a class earn grades of A.

A system such as the one described can be adjusted to be sure that all the normal requirements of the course are met. For example, in a computer science class, it would be expected that the students complete a certain number of programming assignments. The rules for a passing grade might include the requirement that at least five laboratory assignments be satisfactorily completed. "Satisfactorily completed" might mean at least half of the available points for a particular activity or project.

In working with a point system, there is the need to avoid the impression that students are in fact learning a certain percentage of the course material. In part, this can be accomplished by avoiding the use of assignments, quizzes, and tasks which have 100 points as the maximum available.

Experience has shown that a point system does not eliminate competition between students. In some cases, the very best students have competed among themselves to see who could accumulate the highest number of points. There seems to be no reason to discourage this type of performance. One caveat: some students will not do anything that they are not absolutely required to do, and they may expect a teacher to bail them out at the end of the quarter or semester. In fairness to all involved, a teacher may have no alternative but to fail them.

This type of grading system is particularly fruitful in a computer science class because there are a variety of instructional materials that can be made available to students that may not be appropriate for all. For example, an optional activity for a business student might be to work his way through a tutorial on a spreadsheet program and design a record-keeping program for his favorite team. Another student planning to be an elementary school teacher might select a tutorial on LOGO. Both activities have value above and beyond the general course level and neither one requires a great deal of the teacher's time.

It is up to an instructor to explore the alternatives that can be made available to his students. A grading system can be more than just a record of performance; it can set the stage for an environment in which a wide range of other instructional strategies can be implemented.

INSTRUCTIONAL STRATEGIES

Lectures

Although most teachers do not like to admit it, the most common teaching strategy used in a classroom is lecturing. The problem is that, by not admitting to it, many teachers do not plan how they will maximize the lecture approach for learning. In many cases, lecturing amounts to no more than information being presented by the teacher, and copied by students into a notebook. Lecturing is more than just talking about a topic; it requires planning and strategies if it is going to lead to meaningful learning.

For our purposes, lecturing will be defined as those activities by which the instructor controls and presents information to an intended group of learners whose primary role is to accept the information. Borrowing from Broadwell (1980), the characteristics of a good lecturer/teacher is someone who (1) is enthusiastic about teaching; (2) can organize the material; (3) has knowledge of the subject matter; (4) communicates the message in a meaningful way; (5) relates the content to the students; (6) understands his roles as information source and facilitator; and (7) has platform skills that can enhance interest and keep students involved. These qualities can be enhanced through the application of certain skills and procedures to the planning of presentations. Those that might have the most significance for the computer science teacher are presented below.

Advanced Organizers. Ausubel et al. (1978) has demonstrated in a whole host of situations that students learn more when the new information being presented is preceded by a presentation at a higher order of abstraction which creates a conceptual framework into which the more specific information can be organized and anchored. New information can be better acquired and assimilated if it can be tied to appropriate anchoring ideas already held in long-term memory.

This leads to the learning strategy known as advanced organizers; it is particularly helpful in lecturing because it assists in organizing the presentation both for the instructor and the student. In teaching programming there are general concepts that can prove helpful as advanced organizers. For example, the concept of iteration can be used as an advanced organizer for the particulars of the FOR/NEXT loop. Instructors who introduce the syntax of FOR/NEXT without talking about the idea that one of the outstanding features of computers is their ability to repeat a series of commands are losing an opportunity to build on a more general concept, and at the same time increase the opportunity for meaningful learning.

It is the more general concepts or strategies that are transferable to other situations, not the specific knowledge. If a computer science teacher wants to teach problem solving, then he must be committed to teaching the more general strategies and not allow his courses to focus exclusively on the syntax and semantics of a particular language.

Models are useful as advanced organizers, especially if the information can be related to other aspects of the model which has been used to explain prior information. For example, prior to introducing the READ statement, students should be reminded of the memory map—a powerful model when dealing with computers—in which the ideas of different segments of memory are allocated for the system, the program, variables, etc. The specific process focused on would be the way in which a computer takes information stored as a variable and utilizes it within a program. Using this idea the rhetorical question might be asked how information that is embedded in the program would need to go in the memory of the computer in order to become useful and available.

In a series of controlled experiments using the pictorial model of a computer shown in Figure 5.1, Mayer (1982) clearly demon-

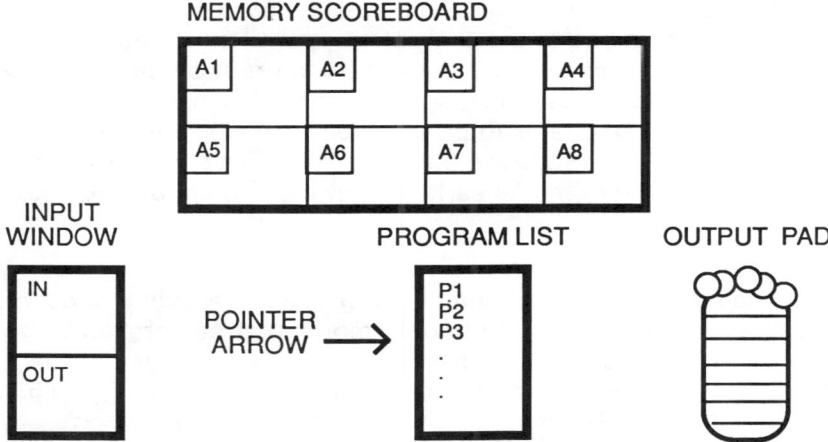

Figure 5.1. *Mayer's Concrete Model of the Computer for a BASIC-like Language*

strated the effectiveness of using the model as an advanced organizer. (See Appendix E for a detailed description of this model.)

Mayer showed repeatedly that using the advanced organizer was effective at enhancing the learner's ability to solve problems which involved transfer. He used the term <u>transfer</u> to indicate problems which were beyond the knowledge level in Bloom's taxonomy. It is interesting to note that when simple recall was tested, those students in the control groups did as well as those using the model. Another observation was that high ability students in the control groups did as well as high ability students in the treatment groups. The latter information suggests that models are not as important to high ability students; an alternate hypothesis is that the high ability students in the control group used their own models or alternative strategies that tended to reduce the need for Mayer's model.

Here is Mayer's conclusion:

These results provide clear and consistent evidence that a concrete model can have a strong effect on the encoding and use of new technical information by novices. These results provide empirical support to the claims that allowing novices to "see the works" allows them to encode in a more coherent and useful way. When appropriate models are used, the learner seems to be able to assimilate each new statement to his or her image of the computer system. Thus, one straightforward implication is: If the goal is to produce learners who will not need to use the language creatively, then no model is needed. If the goal is to produce learners who will be able to come up with creative solutions to novel (for them) problems, then a concrete model early in learning is quite useful (1982, 26).

The model shown in Figure 5.1 was used by Mayer in most of his studies, but it was not the only model that has proven to be useful. In a series of experiments using a file management language, Mayer used a second model which is shown in Figure 5.2 and described in Appendix E.

The features of a model should be based on the commands and structures that are going to be taught. Even though the model will become more elaborate as the concepts to be explained become more advanced, students find it very difficult to discard anything that they have learned. A teacher must make sure that early

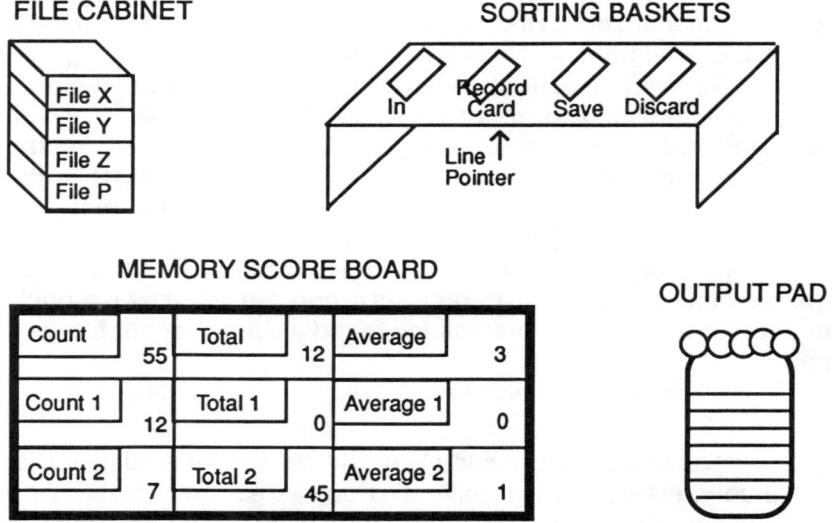

Figure 5.2. Mayer's Concrete Model of the Computer for a SEQUEL-type Language

simplifications do not cause conceptual problems further down the road.

Black Box Versus Glass Box. The idea of using a concrete model for introducing computer concepts was also developed by duBoulay et al. (1976). They suggested that too often teachers use a "black box" approach when teaching about computers. In this approach the student is told not to be concerned about what happens inside the computer, but rather to look at each segment or function as a black box which has a set of inputs, a process and a set of outputs. The process need only be presented in terms of the inputs and outputs without regard to what actually happens in the box. This approach may lead to programs that run, but it will hardly lead to an understanding of how a computer works.

Mayer (1979) argue for the advantages of explaining the process which takes place within the black box using an idealized set of parts. The parts need only be at a level of detail that will allow the processes being considered to be explained at what he calls the "transaction level." This is called the "glass box approach."

This approach suggests that two important properties are needed in the model; (1) simplicity—a small number of parts that interact in a way that can be easily understood, and (2) visibility—novices should be able to imagine the selected parts and processes of the model in action.

As noted by Mayer (1982, 19), it is unfortunate that du Boulay has not provided empirical data to support the effectiveness of using his "LOGO machine" in promoting problem solving as compared to the "traditional" mode of learning LOGO which emphasizes hands-on activities. Keep in mind, the notion of teaching students LOGO using a model would be the antithesis of the exploratory model that its developers have said is the key to its success.

The use of models to add understanding to the workings of a computer is not simply a heuristic technique. Programmers and systems analysts rely on visual models of stacks, pointers, screen locations, links, etc., in order to deal with the complexities of the computer. In the more general scheme of things, the use of models is one of the most powerful tools of science and technology.

This research suggests that a teacher needs to be conscious of each student's learning style, and whether that need might be met to some degree by a computer model that can be used to promote meaningful learning.

Line Table. Another useful approach to helping students follow the sequence of events in a programming segment is to use a line table. A line table shows the systematic change in variables, inputs, and outputs as one precedes through the program line by line. An example can be found in Chapter 2, Figure 2.3.

Commentary. To be a successful lecturer, a teacher needs to be able to make the information presented both meaningful and relevant. One way to do this is to have planned diversions within the lecture which reduce the cognitive load that is placed on the students—high school students cannot absorb the amount of information that can be presented in forty-five minutes of straight lecture. They need an opportunity to place the material into perspective, so the lecturer must use strategies aimed at controlling the flow. Some techniques that are employed are (1) humor; (2) anecdotes; (3) visual aids; and (4) analogies. Each of these will be briefly discussed.

Humor

Surely the most successful diversion in a lecture is humor. A story, a cartoon, or a personal experience that can be drawn upon to make a point or establish a moment of relief. An instructor should be on the watch for jokes or cartoons or experiences that can be tied to specific topics. Although humor is widely known as a positive factor in lectures, a search of the literature on the topic of "humor" shows very few citations, and of them only one was a research report.

In the past ten years, the only study that investigated the effects of humor on student achievement was done by Desberg, Henschel, and Marshall (1981). It showed that for college students, humor related to the content being taught had a significant effect on student learning when compared to groups that were exposed to unrelated humor or a humorless control group. Cazden (1986), in a comprehensive review of the research on classroom discourse, reported the same paucity of references to research on humor. Nevertheless, as most experienced teachers can tell you, a humorless classroom is highly likely to be less productive than one where humor is an integral part of the instruction.

Anecdotes

Students are interested in things that have happened to real people. The history of computer science is a long series of interesting events and circumstances from the first programming by Countess

Lovelace or the coining of the term "bug" by Grace Hopper, to the financing of the original Apple by the sale of a VW bus.

The choice of stories will go a long way in establishing the credibility of the instructor with his/her students, because they will come to know what the teacher thinks is interesting and amusing about the subject and how it fits into the mainstream of their life. Students are often more interested in their teachers as people than the course that they are teaching. The stories that are told can set the tone for this relationship.

Visual Aids

One thing a teacher should keep in mind when he is lecturing to students is that their minds will wander away from the subject at hand. Even if a teacher has their attention to begin with, the presentation is likely to encourage them to think about something other than what the teacher is thinking about. The trick is to bring them back to the flow of the presentation from time to time. This may be achieved through the use of visuals or transparencies.

An outline of the main topics of a presentation, or a diagram showing the major aspects of a model of a complex example help to provide focus and gain attention. Not only is a good set of transparencies helpful in adding order to a presentation, but the use of transparencies has the effect of demonstrating to the students that a teacher has prepared the lesson and is not merely winging it. The preparation of transparencies is no longer the time-consuming task that it once was before the availability of micro-computers; more about that later, under Material Production, later in this chapter.

Analogies

In the presentation of information or concepts to students, the key to learning is linking the new to the known. As stated earlier, Ausubel et al. (1978, iv) has said, "The most important single factor influencing learning is what the learner already knows." When introducing new topics with groups, the diversity of the students' backgrounds and prior experiences makes it difficult to assume singular prior experience or learning, but there are ideas and concepts that can be considered part of their cultural base. Students often have collective knowledge of a wide range of principles and concepts from areas other than that being taught. In some cases, a teacher can build on very simple ideas and point the students in the direction of the new concepts through analogies.

The use of analogies, models, and metaphors is one of the better strategies for instruction because, if the referenced phenomenon is understood and has features which parallel the intended new concept and its features, learning can be facilitated. The simplest analogies are things like mailboxes used to identify memory locations for the storage of variables, as described in Chapter 2. This is an excellent, albeit limited, analogy because almost all students are familiar with mailboxes and the idea that there is a difference between the address of a mailbox and the contents of the mailbox is clear. Care must be used in teaching this analogy lest the student think of the memory location as being like a real mailbox which can hold a variety of mail and more than one letter. Care must be taken in using any analogy to be sure that the student understands the limitations of the analogy. Nevertheless, saying that the memory of a computer is like a set of mailboxes is a useful approach.

It may be recalled that BASIC was developed with the idea that the computer should be invisible to the programmer; Kurtz and Kemeny (1985) proposed that programming should be taught to novices so that the student does not have to be aware of how the machine functions. This is a "black box" analogy. For many students this is not a useful analogy because they lack the concept of a "black box". In those cases, saying that a computer is like a black box is a way of leading into an explanation of what a black box is like, rather than the intended link to prior knowledge or concepts.

As noted above, Mayer (1982) has provided experimental evidence that the use of a concrete model promotes learning of programming. The use of a scoreboard for memory, an input window, a program list and an output pad can contribute to the understanding of a simplified set of machine operations.

The use of simple, direct analogies is not exactly spectacular; however, some teachers fail to use these linkages, and others are careless about defining the limits of the analogies, leading to potential confusion. Analogies can be used at a higher, more abstract level to get at more difficult concepts and ideas of computer science. A very powerful analogy for programming has been suggested by Wirth (1984). He suggests that programming should be viewed as the process of designing a new machine with the aid of an existing, general purpose machine. Programming is like designing a general purpose machine to solve a particular problem.

Rather than viewing the computer as a black box, Wirth would have the programmer produce his own unique machine in detail.

A similar concept, the engineering analogy, was proposed by duBoulay (1986, 60) as being useful in visualizing how a student learns programming. In this analogy, a student is visualized as being in a darkened room where he is building a mechanism that he can only barely see. The student puts together parts to make units without a full understanding of the parts, their functions nor their contributions to the whole. Gradually the light becomes better, the machine starts to make sense, and the parts become part of a machine that can be adjusted, repaired, and fixed to solve more and more complex problems. This particular analogy has power. It addresses not only the operation of the computer, but it defines the role of the student as well.

DuBoulay (1986, 58) suggests that care needs to be taken in the use of analogies. The misapplication of analogy is one of the most common mistakes made by naive programmers. The error arises when a learner tries to extract more structure or relationship from the an analogy than is warranted.

The use of analogies or metaphors is also useful in the teaching of more philosophical aspects of computers and their relationship to man. Turkle (1984) suggests that it is helpful to think of the mind as being like a multiprocessor, and that there is a special linkage between the mind and the computer that makes it different than any other technological development in history.

An extreme form of analogy is the personification of an object so that it takes on the characteristics and qualities of a human being. Whether or not a computer should be made to appear like a human being is certainly a question that can be debated. While it might form a useful instructional link, it could lead to extensions that would be counterproductive. People are fearful that the computer may take on functions that they reserve for themselves; to make computers seem more like people has the effect of approving the transfer of functions to systems that need to be in the hands of people who work within a context of emotions, values and judgments.

The power of analogies has been extended to the user interface of the computer. The Macintosh computer, and now the IBM compatibles through the use of "Windows", were developed around the concept that a computer's operating system might be viewed as a "desktop", with icons representing applications and files, pull-down menus for ease of access, and a pointer for selection. This approach will have an impact on the learning of programming and the development of problem-solving skills, because it will lead to a more efficient introductory learning environment.

Peelle (1983) has provided an interesting review of the use of analogies and metaphors used to teach students about computers. In addition to some of the analogies already mentioned, he draws our attention to additional approaches: the computer as brain, the computer as map, the computer as vitamin, the computer as palette, the computer as mentor, and the computer as catalyst. It is beyond the scope of this text to present each of these metaphors, but the mere suggestion of the images brings ideas to mind, ideas that reinforce the power of metaphors and analogies. An interesting assignment for students is to ask them to develop their own analogy for the computer.

Demonstrations

Lectures are often interspersed with demonstrations; at other times, demonstrations are performed for classes as separate events without the formal lecture. In a demonstration, the key idea is that the students will see whatever is being demonstrated rather than just have an oral presentation or explanation. Numerous things can be demonstrated, but typically a student is shown a copy of a listing and then the listing is run to show what it will or will not do. This, of course, does not preclude the demonstration of hardware or special applications of computers.

From a pedagogical point of view, the demonstration of the outcome of a lesson or unit is very effective. For example, if students are going to do an assignment which would require them to prepare a graphical image on the screen, showing the student some examples of what students have done with this same assignment in the past can be very helpful in promoting interest and competition as well as understanding.

The first rule of demonstration is that every student in the classroom must have an opportunity to see the thing being demonstrated. It is surprising how often a teacher does a demonstration and then needs to describe to the class what is actually happening. This is simply not an acceptable procedure. A demonstration should be exactly that, an opportunity to see what is being shown.

It is essential that if a teacher is going to show students the listing of a program or the actual running of an application, he needs to have some kind of large display or multiple screens. A rule of thumb from the research on classroom viewing of videos says that one inch of diagonal screen size per student viewing a screen is needed. With text material on the screen, this might be the minimum screen size; a more likely estimate would be of the order of 1.5 to 2.0 inches per viewer, and then only if the screens are strategically placed so that no student is more than 15 feet from the screen itself.

The use of large screens, 20 to 30 inches on the diagonal, has been one successful approach, but the mounting of monitors or the use of viewing carts are both expensive outlays. The initial response to this has been the development of large screen projectors. These do provide a viable alternative to monitors, but the cost has limited their use in the K-12 setting. Recent development of adapters for overhead projectors which provide monitor-like images is making the problem less difficult to resolve, and as cost decreases, this will likely be the method of choice.

The problem of projecting computer output for demonstration purposes can be resolved, but teachers need to make it important enough to do. For the short term, if they are confronted with a lack of large scale projection equipment or a viewing area which does not provide easy reading of the screen, the alternative is to provide the students with hardcopy of what is being demonstrated. In many cases, providing hardcopy is helpful so that the student does not have to be concerned about copying text while he is trying to understand the concept or idea being demonstrated. In some cases, when a program is being demonstrated, it is useful to have the source code available for each student so that he can follow the listing as the program is stepped through on the screen.

When software is being demonstrated, it is within the control of the instructor. This is a real advantage because some software that is not particularly user-friendly can still be used on a demo basis. However, it is very important that a teacher practice using a piece of software before demonstrating it to a class. When it is demonstrated, a teacher should be aware of what he is going to demonstrate and of the software's limitations; a beginning teacher needs to avoid the pitfalls of trying to explain an unanticipated event during a demonstration.

Finally, a demonstration should be just that, not an explanation. When something is demonstrated, the teacher must first motivate attention by showing a sincere interest, then make sure that the students have seen the planned object, then make the explanation. The teacher should not be explaining something that has not been seen by the audience.

The rules for demonstrations are simple:

1. Everyone must see what is being demonstrated.
2. The demonstration needs to be practised to avoid unanticipated events.
3. Students should see what is planned before it is explained.

Projects

A computer science student certainly can take advantage of the available technology to do constructive long-term projects. A project is one way to offset the criticism of computer programming classes that by their very nature they limit programming development to short programs which never give a sense of the actual skills required in the software development environment.

The use of long-term projects of a more sophisticated nature, either by individuals or teams, can be a challenging way to extend the classroom experience. The projects can also lead to products that might be useful in the class or to the school in general. The choice of projects is a matter of anticipation and assessment of the participant's skills and ability by the teacher. Possible topics for projects might be:

- Development of a new game.
- Preparation of a tutorial on some aspects of computer programming.
- Construction of an electronic device from a kit.
- Preparation of a data base.

Projects are easier to start than to finish. One way a teacher can facilitate the development of a project is to insist upon a clear set of specifications about the product before work begins, a timeline for major events, and formative evaluation as the project progresses.

A term, or year-long, project can be an excellent way of drawing together the many aspects of a course. It is particularly useful in a course where structured programming is emphasized to have students develop a major programming project in which a team approach is used, and where the final product is a composite of the modules that are developed by individual team members. A team approach has considerable merit because it simulates the actual work environment of software development. Incorporated in a team approach could be a heavy emphasis on the walkthrough concept discussed in Chapter 3.

Computer Clubs

Many schools have computer clubs; they provide an informal atmosphere in which students can pursue their own interests and ideas. They can also provide the highly motivated or advanced student with the opportunity to gain some recognition for outstanding achievement.

A computer club advisor must not take too passive a role lest the club's activities slide into a focus on computer games and copying software. The advisor's primary role should be to provide specific challenges to keep the students' creative energies involved with constructive activities.

Computer clubs can be the source of valuable student help for computer and computer center maintenance. As equipment gets older and systems more complex, the need for routine maintenance and repairs increases. Student help can make the difference between a smooth-running operation and one plagued with a constant series of breakdowns and distractions.

Media

To provide variety, and to address different learning styles in a class, a teacher needs to look to alternative instructional modes and media. It is surprising with all the advances made in the development of instructional materials, that the mainstay of instruction is still the lecture.

CAI: Computer Assisted Instruction. The most obvious medium for the computer science teacher would seem to be the computer itself, but there are very few computer assisted instructional (CAI) programs to teach programming, and those that are available tend to teach only the syntax of the languages rather than the overall concepts and problem-solving techniques. When the objective is to teach syntax, it might be appropriate to use computer assisted instruction. In general, the research on CAI shows that it is an efficient and cost effective way to teach information at the knowledge level (Kearsley et al. 1983a, 1983b).

Textbooks. The most common supplementary instructional material available to the classroom teacher is a textbook. Textbooks and related items have been estimated to be the source of 90% of instruction in schools (Solomon 1978, Carus 1986). Even in an area of the curriculum where hands-on experience is the primary mode of instruction, textbooks are available and widely used. In some districts it is easier to get approval for a textbook than it is to get software because the selection and budgetary processes are in place for approval and purchase of textbooks; software is considered something else.

The selection of a textbook, as with any other instructional material, should be done with a view towards the goals and objectives of the curriculum; all too often a textbook is selected and it then becomes the curriculum. Some critics of our educational system maintain that the textbook publishers are often the real controllers of curriculum.

Selection of a textbook is often done by a districtwide committee. The committee may be assisted by a statewide adoption list which specifies the textbooks that meet the requirements of the state curriculum. Both Texas and California have statewide adoption lists, and because of the number of textbooks sold in each of these states, the publishers tend to favor views of educators in each of these states that might participate in the selection process. The politics of textbook selection is of concern to educators because of the significant role that textbooks play in establishing a de facto national curriculum (Farr and Tulley 1985).

Textbook selection at the local level can be a very formal and complex process, but in some high schools and junior high schools, the choice is left to the individual teacher or department. Whether or not a state has an adoption list is secondary, because a state that does not have an adoption list has little impact on the publishers, while those states which do have adoption lists provide the critical input. This narrows the choices for other states.

The impact of a state adoption process is presented by Westley (1986) in her discussion of the selection of computer literacy textbooks for the junior high curriculum in Texas. Texas mandated that in the 1985–86 school year all students would need to pass a one-semester computer literacy course. The course was to include a variety of topics including the use of computers as tools, societal issues, and ethics. Although the role of programming was limited, the guidelines specified that the programming language was to be BASIC at the junior high level.

The result of these guidelines was that twelve publishers developed textbooks for this market, and all twelve included BASIC.

It is unlikely that there will be any textbook written for the junior high level which will not include BASIC as the programming language of choice. The Texas textbook adoption process has led to de facto standardization of the junior high computer literacy curriculum.

It is likely that over the next few years, one or two textbooks will become, de facto, the available texts because there is a limited number of publishers that are capable of developing the marketing strategies to impact the market. The present situation is that there are few textbooks vying for the high school market.

The selection of a computer science textbook must take into account all the standards used in selecting any textbook, but should include other features which are of specific interest to the computer science classroom. The following special considerations need to be considered:

1. Does the textbook integrate well with the software that is to be used?
2. Does the textbook and/or software require specialized training?
3. Is special adaptive hardware and/or specific software required?
4. Can the software be easily managed? Can it be networked?
5. Will the software require much teacher maintenance?
6. Are there licensing fees?

An excellent review of computer literacy textbooks has been done by Boudrot and Switzer (1986). Their presentation was part of the adoption process that took place in Texas. Although tied to specific learning and planning objectives, the details and commentary form an excellent basis for anyone considering a study of computer textbooks. The review includes the five books that were subsequently adopted by the state of Texas. It also includes the general format, stated goals, and summaries of the text (number of pages by topics), teacher's guide, and supplementary materials. The evaluation includes strengths and weaknesses and an overall summary. Each publisher was also provided an opportunity to respond to the review.

This review exemplifies the amount of work that enters into the textbook selection process. Because the review is tied to the Texas curriculum, it should only be used with caution in other states with different goals and objectives for their computer literacy courses. Then there is the obvious problem of the information becoming outdated as the textbooks are updated and new books are published.

Textbook selection is important because all too frequently once a textbook is selected, the teacher is "stuck" with it for a period of at least five years, and often longer.

Sample Programs. One of the weaknesses of many introductory programming texts is that they offer very few examples of completed and well-documented programs. It is simply too expensive and awkward to insert lengthy segments of code within the body of a textbook. If a certain level of performance is expected of students, it is reasonable to have the same expectation of the materials that they are shown. Student performance increases when they are shown examples of the terminal behavior expected of them. One approach to this is to keep a collection of student assignments or projects that can be reviewed by students.

Films/Video. Films and video tapes have not been accorded the academic respectability they might deserve. In the past, films and videos have typically been used as something extra or as a filler, often with little bearing on the actual curriculum.

The problem with films and videos is that they tend to be very general, and contain more information than can be assimilated at the rapid pace presented. By the same token, a film can be very useful in presenting an overview or summarizing a unit, but it is not reasonable to expect a film or video to teach something on its own.

A significant roadblock to the use of films and videos has been the scheduling of the media for the classroom. Some districts require that films be scheduled as much as a year in advance for a particular show date. Even the most experienced teacher has trouble projecting a schedule that far in advance. A film that arrives two days early or two days late is difficult to blend into an instructional plan. This problem is decreasing as video tapes are becoming less expensive, and it is becoming practical for schools to own their own copies rather than relying on central collections or rental agencies.

The use of video cassettes in the computer science classroom has been facilitated because frequently the same monitors that are used to project computer programs can be used to present video images. Video cassettes also have advantage over films in that short segments can be isolated and played more conveniently than is the case with films.

CLASSROOM MANAGEMENT

Physical Arrangements. The selection of a classroom for a computer laboratory is an important step in planning for instruction. Sales (1985) has provided an excellent discussion of the many variables to be taken into account. A well-designed facility will encourage use by students and teachers; a poorly designed room can have a negative impact. He suggests the following guidelines for selecting a location:

- The room should be large enough to meet the requirements of the additional space required of computers.
- The room should be free of partitions and dividers.
- The room should be centrally located to provide convenient access.
- The room should not receive direct sunlight.

The design of a computer laboratory is a major factor in the management of a programming environment. As already noted, the preference for a laboratory with separate computer stations and classroom seating provides some advantages because of the flexibility it provides in delivering instruction. Unfortunately most schools do not have rooms of sufficient size to do all that would be desirable.

Sales also suggests some very practical ideas for the preparation of a classroom:

- Walls should be covered with low-gloss paint to reduce reflections.
- Lighting should be indirect or recessed.
- Storage space is needed: shelving, cabinets, and locked areas.
- Boards should be dust free; traditional black boards need to be avoided.
- Electrical circuits should be isolated from other circuits, particularly those associated with heavy-duty equipment.
- Electrical outlets should be sufficient to take into account the number of computers, printers, monitors, and other equipment that will be required.
- A master switch should provide control over all hardware. (If students are to be seated at their workstation for instruc-

tion, a separate master switch might be installed for a separate monitor circuit.)
- A separate control should be provided to control the lighting level.
- A private telephone line or lines should be installed for telecommunications.
- Temperature control should be independent of other areas.

It is possible to include most of these recommendations when a room is being built or renovated; they could be prohibitively expensive once a center is in operation. It seems that most computer science teachers spend so much energy getting together the resources to provide the hardware for a computer laboratory that they tend to neglect the ambience.

This neglect is most evident in the design of the actual work area. It is common practice to place computers on tables that were designed for study halls or cafeterias, with wires running this way and that to the available outlets. Computers are arranged around the perimeter of the room solely to avoid wiring problems. Often very little attention is given to the comfort of the students.

The design of a workstation has received considerable interest in the "real world" of home and office. There is considerable information available on the ergonomics of the computer workstation. Articles appear on a regular basis in periodicals for the data processing manager and the home hobbyist, but computer education magazines tend to neglect the topic.

In designing a computer workstation, the most significant concern should be the height of the keyboard, and its relationship to the actual work surface. A typical table or desk top would be at 29", while the proper height of a keyboard would be between 26" and 28" for proper typing position. Ideally, the keyboard surface should be adjustable for both height and angle to provide maximum comfort for the user.

In a classroom or laboratory, the workstation should include room for books, an area for printouts, and writing space. If the computers are to used by two students at a time, then added space needs to be provided in the work area. Other factors that might be considered in the design of a student workstation are adjustable chairs, the distance and angle of the screen from the user, and provisions for supervision.

Scheduling. The location of computer workstations in a school determines their availability and potential amount of use. Becker's survey (1986b) showed that computers received more use when they were located in separate computer laboratories versus classrooms or the library. Most computer science teachers would prefer to have a classroom with their own computers which would be available any time they wanted the students to enter programs, but computers are too expensive a resource to be the exclusive tools of an individual teacher. Although there might be only one computer science teacher in a high school, that teacher would be teaching more than computer science classes, and besides, computers need to be available for other uses. There is an increasing demand for computers to be used in creative writing classes, and as an instructional tool in science, social studies and other classes.

Even in a computer science classroom, the computers would not be used all the time. A good approximation would be that the computers would be in use less than fifty percent of the time, even in a course that had a high priority on programming. Students who are stationed at a workstation all the time that they are in class will be getting the message that programming is done in the interactive mode rather than through well-designed plans. The better message is that the time at the keyboard is for entering and debugging code which has been planned, written out, and approved before sitting down at the keyboard.

Whenever possible, a separate room should be set aside for computer workstations, and the room should be scheduled so as to provide for priority access by those needing maximum usage. There should be provisions for others to use the equipment.

Media Control. The management of a set of microcomputers and the related software requires thought and skill. In some classes, teachers assign books to students on the first day of class, and the next thing they have to manage is the collection of the books at the end of the semester. Of course, there is the day-to-day collection and distribution of assignments. For the computer science teacher this can be a time-consuming hassle or the key to a well-orchestrated flow of students into a class.

There are many ways that the process may be managed, but a simple and effective way is to have a disk for each student that remains in the classroom at all times. When the student enters the room on a day that the computers are going to be used, which could be every day, he takes his disk from the classroom box and proceeds to his assigned computer and begins work. Students can be working on the computers while the teacher takes care of other housekeeping chores, such as greeting students, recording attendance, making announcements, returning assignments, etc. Not only does this avoid the loss of student time waiting to get to the instructional part of the class, but some students will come to class early to get in extra time on a computer.

Once the "extras" are taken care of, the students can be directed to return to their regular classroom seats for instruction and discussion. If possible, students should not receive instruction while they are sitting in front of an active video screen. Not all teachers would agree, but the terminal can create a significant distraction when a teacher is trying to instruct.

At the end of the class, each student returns his/her disk to the class file. In this scheme, it is wise to have each student retain his own copy of his disk which he takes with him. This disk serves as a backup, and it should be brought to every class, but it is not essential for smooth running of the class.

A teacher might have up to five classes of students, which could mean as many as a hundred and twenty-five students. The task of sorting and reviewing that many disks can be unmanageable to the point that student programs may not be reviewed. A procedure that can be followed is to have an "assignment disk" for each class on which all programs are placed that are to be reviewed by the instructor. Having a single disk per class, and having a student's name as part of the program title, can be very efficient.

All of this disk managing can be reduced with networking and a file server, but keep in mind this means that in order to read students' programs, the teacher needs to have access to the hard disk. Some of the convenience of getting the student programs into a single location is offset by the instructor needing to grade the programs at this same location.

Special Access. Students with special needs should be considered in the planning for a computer laboratory. Placing a computer center on a second floor without a elevator, using a room with a narrow doorway, or having a room that is so small that the aisle is restricted; all can eliminate the use of the lab by the physically handicapped. Being required to have access and in fact having access that is convenient are two different things.

Not only do the physical features and location of a center have a special significance for the handicapped, but the design of the workstations themselves may be problematic. Although regular students benefit from keyboard heights that are less than table top height, wheelchairs typically will not fit under anything less than tabletop height; normal height is better, adjustable height is best.

Workstations for the handicapped should also have more tabletop area to provide for adaptive devices, and to provide space for an aide or assistant to work with them when necessary. It is also desirable to have computers with detachable keyboards. Although there is more adaptive equipment available for the Apple computers, the Apple II series presented an obstacle for many students because the keyboard was attached to the CPU. Physically orienting a computer for ready access by a student with physical limitations can be a real problem.

Teachers should not be shy about asking a student's occupational or physical therapist to assist in adjusting a computers environment for a special student. A wiggling body on the floor, pecking out a message with a mouthwand, on a computer keyboard propped up with a couple of pillows, may not be a scenario for an orderly lab, but it could be just the right prescription for a student with muscular dystrophy. Wheeling a student into the lab is just a first step in providing access.

MATERIAL PRODUCTION

Having access to the computer gives the computer science teacher the opportunity to utilize many applications packages that can assist him in the preparation of instructional materials. Using the technology can give a clear message to students that computers are accepted as an ordinary part of the workplace.

One of the simplest but most effective uses of computers is the preparation of transparency masters. A problem with preparing transparency masters in the past has been that typed copy was too small to give an image that would be visible on the overhead projector. The minimum size for a transparency image to be used in a classroom is 14 points, and 18 points is probably average. A typewriter is limited to 12 points. The alternatives were to prepare the copy freehand or to use rub-on letters. The first required a skill that many teachers do not have; the latter required more time and money than the average teacher was willing to commit. There are a variety of programs that can be used to get large lettering, and often they provide options for style and layout.

The computer can also be used to prepare all sorts of students materials—worksheets, laboratory exercises, sample listings—which can enhance the teaching process. For example, students can be provided with excellent drill and practice exercises in the form of crossword puzzles generated with the use of a program called Crossword Magic (1981). The advantage of teacher-generated student worksheets is that they can be tied directly to the instructional program and not include extraneous subject matter as is often the case with published materials.

One of the more effective tools for a teacher is the gradebook software that is available. Unlike the traditional gradebook which was a teacher's private domain, electronic gradebooks can be used to provide weekly printouts of grades, lists of missing assignments, and parent notes. Complicated grading systems can be employed in which grades are used for ongoing motivation. Not only do electronic gradebooks provide for better feedback to students, but they can save a teacher a good deal of time in dealing with the records of a hundred or more students.

COMMENTARY

There is growing support for the notion that teachers would be more successful in the classroom if only they had better knowledge of their subject matter. Certainly the trend is towards more thorough academic preparation of teachers at the expense of instruction in methods of teaching and clinical supervision. Several states now have programs which allow college graduates to enter the classroom as interns with minimum or no preparation in pedagogy.

This is an area of honest debate and differences of opinion. The problem of teachers trying to teach courses in which they have little or no academic preparation has almost been hidden from the public, which finances our schools. There was a period of time in which it was thought that methods were more important than content, and that any teacher with a credential in one subject area had the right to teach any subject area. Strong union contracts provided job protection that led to teachers teaching outside their areas of expertise. The educational bureaucracy is slow to acknowledge the extent to which high school teachers are poorly prepared to teach outside their subject matter. Declining school enrollments, low salaries, and a general trend away from the value of academic skills have impacted our schools; there is a lack of teachers in general, and a tremendous lack of teachers in certain critical areas, including teachers of computer science.

The point is that, although this chapter, and this book in total, focuses on methods for teaching computer science, unless the teachers are competent in the subject matter areas they teach, the methods are irrelevant. On the other hand, knowing the content is not sufficient; a teacher needs to develop a set of methods that bridge the gap between the instructor's knowledge and the students' ignorance.

The key to using methods is planning. A teacher needs to attend to sequence and to style, to pace and to focus, to context and to detail. A teacher needs to develop a repertoire of methods, some based on research, others on experience, and still others on a sense of the capabilities of students. But the single most important task is the planning that is required to put all the components together into a meaningful learning experience for students.

RECOMMENDED READINGS

Gregory C. Sales, "Design Considerations for Planning a Computer Classroom." *Educational Technology*, Vol. 25, No. 5, May 1 985, pp. 7–13. A very thorough presentation on the design of a room as a computer laboratory. The single best source on the topic.

Martin M. Broadwell, *The Lecture Method of Instruction: The Instructional Design Library* , Volume 27, Educational Technology Publications, Englewood Cliffs, New Jersey, 1980. Although lecturing is the most prevalent mode of instruction in the schools, there is very little information available on the planning and delivery of lectures. This book provides a process for preparing a lecture and some thoughtful considerations to take into account to provide the best setting.

SUGGESTED ACTIVITIES

1. Prepare a report which compares the objectives of an introductory course as recommended by ACM with an advanced placement course as recommended by the College Board (Appendix D).

2. Interview a computer science teacher with the purpose of

determining how he meets the needs of special or gifted children in his computer science program.

3. Prepare a quiz of between 5 and 10 multiple choice or short answer questions which would assess students' knowledge of one of the following areas:

- Top-down design
- Recursion
- Nesting of FOR/NEXT loops
- Argument passing
- Pseudocode

4. Prepare a set of transparency masters that could be used to explain the analogy of computer as brain.

5. Prepare the handout that you would use for your first laboratory (programming) assignment in a class of novice high school programmers.

APPENDIX A
Certification Standard for Computer Science National Association of State Directors of Teacher Education and Certification

STANDARD I   The program shall require demonstrated competence in problem-solving methods and algorithm development, analysis, and application.

STANDARD II   The program shall require demonstrated competency in three widely-used, high-level, structured programming languages.

STANDARD III   The program shall require demonstrated competence in the techniques of program design, documentation, and debugging.

STANDARD IV   The program shall require demonstrated competence in the programming, discipline, and design for large programs.

STANDARD V   The program shall require demonstrated competence in string processing, recursion, and internal search/sort methods.

STANDARD VI   The program shall require demonstrated competence in basic concepts of computer systems, computer architecture, and assembly language.

STANDARD VII   The program shall require demonstrated competence in organization of computer languages to include run-time behaviors of programs and the formal study of programming language specification and analysis.

STANDARD VIII   The program shall require demonstrated competence in data structures to include design techniques of non-numeric algorithms which act on data structures.

STANDARD IX   The program shall require demonstrated competence in the design criteria for the selection of methods for data manipulation in the environment of a data base management system.

APPENDIX B
DOCUMENTATION GUIDELINES TENINO HIGH SCHOOL TENINO, WASHINGTON

DOCUMENTATION

The purpose of documentation in computer programming is to present the user of a program with an understanding of how a program works. It is the desire of the original programmer to provide the user, or another programmer who might be interested in modifying the program, with sufficient information to make modifications without redoing the code entirely.

In programming for microcomputers, we will assert that it is good practice to include as much information internally as possible so that potential users will not have to depend on paper copy that often gets separated from the disks.

It is also asserted that the programmer has a responsibility to communicate his procedures and techniques to the user, and that convoluted or hidden processes are inappropriate.

The first level of documentation requires that a program be separated into logical segments; each segment performing a specific task, and characterized by a single entry point and a single exit point. A segment might be called a module. Each segment is identified by a header with a clearly defined descriptive title in the following format:

```
1000  REM
1010  REM    *****************************
1020  REM           MAIN MENU
1030  REM    *****************************
1040  REM
```

A program would typically be constructed as a series of segments; each segment would have its own heading. Please note the blank lines preceding and following the character string line.

This format makes it easy to locate desired segments when working through a listing of a program whether it be on the screen or in hard copy.

The second level of documentation is a description or explanation of the segment or module. Although some headings are clear enough not to require further explanation, some headings require several lines of text in order to communicate their function. For example, the previous heading might be followed by this comment:

```
1050   REM    THE MAIN MENU PROVIDES THE
1060   REM    ENTRY TO THE PROGRAM. THE
1070   REM    USER DECIDES WHETHER HE IS
1080   REM    GOING TO ENTER NEW DATA OR
1090   REM    DO SOMETHING WITH THE
1100   REM    INFORMATION ALREADY IN THE
1110   REM    FILE.
```

A good comment will explain the general flow of the program. A comment is not required after each heading because many times the code is self-explanatory. Of course, what is very clear to one programmer might not be all that clear to another. When in doubt, include a comment. It should be noted that the above comment has been written so that it can be readily read by the user—there are no split words or wrapping around of text.

Frequently, a particular section of a module or segment contains an unusual sequence of steps. It is appropriate to include a comment statement at any such point. The comment should be before the complex code.

The third level of internal documentation is related to the identification of specific variables, procedures or programming lines which warrant special attention. Here again the remark statement is used. In this case, the remark is typically incorporated in the programming statement that needs clarification. For example, if a new variable is defined or used for the first time, it should be identified, as:

```
500 LET A1 = N − 2: REM A1 = COUNT OF
        POSSIBLE ALTERNATIVES
```

In addition to the three levels of internal documentation, it is considered good programming practice to define all variables and arrays at the beginning of the listing of a program. This practice has many advantages, not the least of which is to avoid the problem of having the same name used for two different variables. It will be our practice to have all variables listed and defined at the beginning of a program, and each variable identified again where it is used in the program for the first time. In any case, the purpose of the documentation is to communicate to the intended user as much information as required to understand the logic and limitations of the program. As might be expected, remark (REM) statements can slow down the running of a program, and they do use up memory. The addition of the documentation being requested in this course can effect the performance of a program. It should be noted that utility programs are available that remove all REM statements from a program listing. Some programmers prefer to have a documented copy of their work and a stripped-down version for actual use. This is an acceptable procedure, but do be careful not to use remark (REM) line numbers as destinations for jump (GOTO and GOSUB) commands.

APPENDIX C
STRUCTURING BASIC

The foremost advocate and defender of BASIC is Arthur Luehr-mann. In 1984, he wrote a series of articles for <u>Creative Computing</u> in which he responded to the critics and offered an alternative: "Structured Programming in Basic" (1984a, b, c, d). Luehrmann argued that BASIC was the common language of almost all self-taught programmers, and it was the language being taught to almost 90% of children in schools. There was no point in thinking that the language was something that could be ignored by the academic computer scientists, and besides, the faults with BASIC were really faults with the programmers and teachers of program-mers, not with the language itself.

He pointed out that the major features of good programming form and structure could be achieved using BASIC by a consistent application of top-down design principles and the utilization of control structures.

For teaching top-down design, he suggested the following sequence.

1. Always start with a simple main routine. Use English phrases to describe the major tasks to be done. Avoid think-ing about details.
2. Translate each English phrase into one or two BASIC state-ments. If more are needed, use a GOSUB statement that refers to a subroutine that will contain the details.
3. Write skeleton versions of the subroutines, including PRINT statements for debugging. Run the program and check that things are done in the right order.
4. Fill in the details of each subroutine. Use these same four steps with each subroutine. If new, more detailed subrou-tines are created in the process, do the same four steps with them.
5. After the program is working according to the original plan, undertake any refinements thought to be necessary or de-sirable.

In a similar fashion, he addressed the steps necessary for the development of proper utilization of control blocks:

1. When writing a program module, avoid thinking about what kind of statement to write next.
2. Instead, decide what kind of control block will be needed: an action block, a loop block, or a branch block.
3. Using a mixture of BASIC and English, write the outline of the appropriate block.
4. Fill in the body of the outline by converting English to BASIC. If the body of the outline calls for nesting another control block inside the present one, repeat these same four steps with the inner block.
5. When the plan is complete, enter and debug the program module.

These guidelines, with the discussion and examples that surrounded them, provided a basis for a defense of BASIC as an appropriate introductory language for the pre-college environment. The material was incorporated in a very popular computer book (Luehrmann and Peckham 1986) used in many schools: Computer Literacy—A Hands-On Approach.

• Modified BASIC: The simplest approach to providing structured programming is to require students to follow certain rules of styles. The rules make the students aware of the needs for structure, and they lead to modular programs.

Each program is viewed as being made up of a set of independent blocks or modules. A useful set of rules for a module might be:

1. A module is a program segment which performs one, and only one, operation.
2. A module is set off from the remainder of the program by specific markers.
3. Each module includes a title and a description of its function.
4. The number of lines in a module is limited to what can be viewed on the screen of the computer.
5. A module has one entry point and one exit point.
6. When possible, a module should be set up as a subroutine.
7. Nonconditional jumps are limited or prohibited between modules.

This is an easy set of rules to enforce; it can help produce organized and understandable code. pseudocode, and walk-throughs, to further the development of good programming style by novices.

The following is an example of what a simple program might look like using the modified or structured approach to BASIC:

```
10    REM  *****************************
20    REM  *                           *
30    REM  *     PROGRAM FOR            *
40    REM  *     CONVERTING             *
50    REM  *     FARHENHEIT             *
60    REM  *     TO CENTIGRADE          *
70    REM  *     TEMPERATURE            *
80    REM  *                           *
90    REM  *       JOE SMITH            *
100   REM  *     13 OCTOBER 1988        *
110   REM  *                           *
120   REM  *****************************
130   REM
140   REM  *****************************
150   REM            VARIABLES
160   REM  *****************************
170   REM
180   REM  F = FAHRENHEIT TEMP
190   REM  C = CELSIUS TEMP
200   REM
500   REM  *****************************
510   REM           MAIN PROGRAM
520   REM  *****************************
530   REM
540   REM  OBTAIN FAHRENHEIT
550   REM  TEMPERATURE
560   GOSUB 1000
570   REM  CONVERT TO CELSIUS
580   GOSUB 2000
590   REM  PRINT CELSIUS
600   REM  TEMPERATURE
610   GOSUB 3000
620   END
1000  REM  *****************************
1010  REM              INPUT
1020  REM  *****************************
```

```
1030  REM
1040  REM  CLEAR SCREEN AND
1050  REM  SET CURSOR
1060  HOME: VTAB 4
1070  INPUT "WHAT FAHRENHEIT
TEMPERATURE DO YOU WANT TO CONVERT TO
CELSIUS?; F
1080  RETURN
2000  REM
2010  REM  *****************************
2020  REM                PROCESS
2030  REM  *****************************
2040  REM
2050  LET C = (F - 32) * (5/9)
2060  RETURN
3000  REM
3010  REM  *****************************
3020  REM                OUTPUT
3030  REM  *****************************
3040  REM
3050  PRINT "THE CELSIUS TEMPERATURE IS";
C
3060  RETURN
```

This same program will be used to illustrate the other options presented below.

• BASIC Templates: Harvey (1986) has approached the problem of teaching structured programming by using standard forms of BASIC and providing the students with templates that serve as guides or skeletons for the development of programs. This procedure relieves the novice of having to learn how to design the overall structure of a program while learning to write code.

In a more typical course, a student would be asked to prepare short trivial programs while learning syntax and how to use an editor. Templates allow the student to begin work dealing with a segment of a larger program. The modeling of a more representative approach to programming is desirable because it brings the student into contact with computer science as it is practiced at the very beginning; the process of structuring might be as important as the product if the student is to become a sophisticated computer user.

Harvey's general form for a program is as follows:

```
0     REM BRANCH TO MAIN PROGRAM
1     GOTO 50000
10    REM STRUCTURED PROGRAM OUTLINE
20    REM FRAMCIS A. HARVEY
30    REM SEPTEMBER 24,1985
40    REM EDT 492-12
50    REM THIS PROGRAM OUTLINE
60    REM TO BE USED FOR ALL PROGRAMS
1000  REM FIRST PROCEDURE
1010  REM (Insert code for first procedure in
lines 1020-  1990)
1992  RETURN
2000  REM SECOND PROCEDURE
2010  REM (Insert code for second procedure in
lines 2020- 2990)
2992  RETURN
3000  REM THIRD PROCEDURE
3010  REM (Insert code for third procedure in
lines 3020-3990)
3992  RETURN
4000  REM ETC.
50000 REM MAIN PROGRAM BEGINS
50010 REM EXECUTE FIRST PROCEDURE
50020 GOSUB 1000
50030 REM EXECUTE SECOND PROCEDURE
50040 GOSUB 2000
50060 GOSUB 3000
63000 REM END OF MAIN PROGRAM
63010 END
```

This may not seem that significant a modification, but the results can be quite startling. The students learn very quickly to organize their programs in intelligent ways, and the concepts of structured programming become clear through the model. Experience has shown that students using templates learn to deal with significant programming tasks—programs that require in excess of one hundred lines of code—much more readily than those taught without the aid of a format guide or template. The template shown above is only one of several that is presented in Harvey's article.

Using templates as a guide, the following would be what the

same temperature conversion program as shown under Modified
BASIC:

```
0     REM BRANCH TO MAIN PROGRAM
1     GOTO 6000
10    REM TEMPERATURE CONVERSION
20    REM PAT MCINTYRE
30    REM 13 OCTOBER 1988
40    REM EDT 492-12
1000  REM        INPUT PROCEDURE
1010  REM CLEAR SCREEN AND
1020  REM SET CURSOR
1030  HOME: VTAB 4
1040  INPUT "WHAT FAHRENHEIT
TEMPERATURE DO YOU WANT TO CONVERT TO
CELSIUS?; F
1050  RETURN
2000  REM        SECOND PROCEDURE
2010  REM        PROCESS PROCEDURE
2020  LET C = (F = 32) * (5/9)
2030  RETURN
3000  REM        OUTPUT PROCEDURE
3010  PRINT "THE CELSIUS TEMPERATURE IS ";
C
3020  RETURN
6000  REM        MAIN PROGRAM BEGINS
6010  REM        EXECUTE INPUT
6020  GOSUB 1000
6030  REM        EXECUTE PROCESS
6040  GOSUB 2000
6050  REM        EXECUTE OUTPUT
6060  GOSUB 3000
6070  REM        ETC.
6300  REM        END OF MAIN PROGRAM
6310  END
```

• Structured BASIC Development System (SBDS): Karl Jahns
(1985) has developed an unusually powerful option to the problem
of teaching structured BASIC using Microsoft BASIC. Rather than
having students restricted by the limitations of the editor and structures available with Applesoft BASIC, his system has the students

write their programs with an editor which is essentially a word processor with functions that provide a structured format. The student does not actually program in BASIC, but rather uses a preprocessor which makes use of the BASIC available on the computer, but under conditions which favor developing a structured program.

The system is part of an approach which focuses on planning and programming techniques that have been found to be efficient among computer programmers, but are often neglected in the teaching of computer science. The program uses pseudocode in English, entered via the editor (word processor) during the planning stages. The pseudocode is transformed by the programmer into programming commands including some non-Applesoft commands.

The editing mode, which is essentially a word processor, provides spacing and indentation common to structured languages such as PASCAL or Forth. The editor comes very close to meeting ANSI standards. The translator, which converts the pseudocode into Applesoft BASIC, supports commands such as SelectCase, Do/While, Do/Until, Case, and If/Then/Else even though these commands are not available in Applesoft BASIC. In addition, subroutines can be called by name, and the entire program is created without line numbers. The SBDS editor performs some housekeeping functions—printing code, saving code, loading code, cataloging disk, etc.—which are menu driven and lead to economies of time and effort.

An example of "source code" in the SBDS is shown below. This is what the student would write in the editor. Step 1 is pseudocode written in English; there is no required syntax but phrases are more convenient to use than actual sentences.

Step 1: Preparation of Master Program in Pseudocode

PROGRAM   Celsius Conversion

Clear Screen and put a title at top
Ask for Fahrenheit temperature in degrees
Convert to Celsius
Display the results

The student would input the lines above using the editor. This stage indicates that the program will be made up of four segments or modules. In Step 2, each functional element of the master program is configured as a subroutine call with a title. The syntax here is limited, but essential. Note the absence of line numbers, and the spacing and indentation.

Step 2: Writing Master Program in BASIC

PROGRAM   Celsius Conversion

```
Call Title        'Clear Screen and put a title at top
Call Input        'Ask for Fahrenheit degrees
Call Convert      'Convert to Celsius
Call Display      'Display the results
End
```

This is done in the editor and requires a minimum of coding. At this point the general structure of the program has been determined. The master program is going to be made up of four subroutine calls. It should be noted that upper and lower case can be used, and that the CALL command uses the names of subroutines rather than line numbers as is customary in most forms of Microsoft BASIC.

Step 3: Writing Skeleton Subroutines

PROGRAM   Celsius Conversion

```
Sub Title   'Clear Screen and put a title at top
    PRINT "Title"
    End sub

Sub Input   'Ask for Fahrenheit degrees
    PRINT "What is the Fahrenheit temperature?"
    End sub

Sub Convert   'Convert to Celsius
    PRINT "Convert"
    End sub

Sub Display   'Display the results
    Print "The Celsius temperature is"
    End sub
```

In the third step, the various pseudo components are added. The program can be translated (using a utility that is provided and accessed through the same menu as the editor) and run at this time, although in this case it obviously does not yield anything but a series of statements. The advantage of this is that as the final coding is done, the program can be translated and run as each segment is added; the total program is not required for execution.

Step 4 is to code each of the subroutines, and check them one by one. An example of what the first subroutine would look like in its final form in the editor is shown below:

Step 4: Writing Details of Subroutines

Sub Title   'Clear Screen and put a title at top
   HOME
   VTAB 5
   PRINT "Fahrenheit to Celsius Conversion"
End sub

It is now necessary to add standard BASIC commands and code, although the syntax is less restrictive. The editor can accept some commands not available in Applesoft BASIC. The translator converts them to acceptable code before execution, but the programmer does not have to be concerned about this. The process is similar to compiling a language, but the system is operating at a much higher level. The "object code" is actually an Applesoft BASIC program with all its limitation, but the "source code" is written in a format that closely resembles ANSI BASIC with features such as CALL, IF/THEN/ELSE, DO/WHILE.

Using SBDS, a student prepares a program plan in pseudocode which is then translated into BASIC commands—the source code—before the translator prepares the final version in standard Applesoft BASIC, "object code." The object code is generally not available to the student, all editing is done in the editor which takes advantage of the word processing capabilities of the system. This is more than just a simulation of a compiler because the source code includes features not available in standard Applesoft BASIC.

A major tradeoff in this approach is that students must learn to use the editor before they can write a program. This is becoming less and less of a problem because so many students have experience with word processors before taking a programming course; students who have worked with word processors are often frustrated by the limited capabilities of BASIC editors. On the positive side, the students write self-documenting code without the complications of line numbers, edit using a word processor, and has available additional control functions that are not typical of BASIC for the microcomputer.

This system may seem complex for high school students, but the program is regularly used at the junior high school level with good success. Instructors report that they are able to teach students to write meaningful programs in as much as a third less time than it normally took using the standard approach.

Appendix D
Advanced Placement Computer Science[1]

Topic Outline

I. Programming methodology
  A. Specification
    1. Problem definition and requirements
    2. Functional specifications for programs
  B. Design
    1. Modularization
    2. Top-down versus bottom-up methodologies
    3. Stepwise refinement of modules and data structures
  C. Coding
    1. Structure
    2. Style, clarity of expression
  D. Program correctness
    1. Testing
      a) Relation to design and coding
      b) Generation of test data
      c) Top-down versus bottom-up testing of modules
    2. Verification
      a) Assertions and invariants
      b) Reasoning about programs
    3. Debugging
  E. Documentation
II. Features of programming languages
  A. Type and declarations
    1. Block structure

[1]James S. Braswell, *Advanced Placement Computer Science*, Mathematic Teacher, Vol. 77, No. 5, May, 1984, pp. 372–379

2. Scope of identifiers
   a) Local identifiers
   b) Global identifiers
B. Data
  1. Constants
  2. Variables
C. Expressions and assignments
  1. Operators and operator precedence
  2. Standard functions
  3. Assignment statements
D. Control structures
  1. Sequential execution
  2. Conditional execution
  3. Iteration (loops or repetitive execution)
E. Input and output
  1. Terminal input and output
  2. File input and output
F. Subprograms
  1. Procedures and functions
  2. Parameters
   a) Actual and formal parameters
   b) Value and reference parameters
  3. Recursion
G. Program annotation
  1. Comments
  2. Indentation and formatting
III. Data types and structures
A. Primitive data types
  1. Numeric data
   a) Floating-point real numbers
   b) Integers
  2. Character (symbolic) data
  3. Logical (Boolean) data
B. Linear data structure
  1. Arrays
  2. Strings
  3. Linked lists
  4. Stacks
  5. Queues
C. Tree structures
  1. Terminology
   a) Nodes: root, leaf, parent, child, sibling

b) Branches and subtrees

c) General tree structures (optional)

D. Representation of data structures

  1. Sequential representation of linear structures

  2. Pointers and linked data structures

IV. Algorithms

  A. Classes of algorithms

    1. Sequential algorithms

    2. Iteration or enumerative algorithms

    3. Recursive algorithms

  B. Searching

    1. Sequential (linear) search

    2. Binary search

    3. Hash-code search

    4. Searching an ordered binary tree

    5. Linear versus logarithmic searching times

  C. Sorting

    1. Selection sort

    2. Onsertion sort

    3. Exchange or bubble sort

    4. Merge sort

    5. Sorting using an ordered binary tree

    6. Quicksort (optional)

    7. Radix sort (optional)

    8. Quadratic versus n*log (n) sorting time

  D. Numerical algorithms

    1. Approximations

      a) Zeroes of functions by bisection

      b) Monte Carlo techniques

      c) Area under a curve (optional)

    2. Statistical algorithms

      a) Measures of central tendency

      b) Measures of dispersion

  E. Manipulation of data structures

    1. String processing

      a) Concatenation

      b) Substring extraction

      c) Matching

    2. Insertion and deletion in linear structures, trees

    3. Tree traversals

V. Application of computing

  A. Text processing

     1. Editors
     2. Text formatters
  B. Simulations and modeling
     1. Continuous simulation of physical processes
     2. Discrete simulation of probabilistic events
  C. Data analysis
     1. Statistical packages
     2. Graphical display of data
  D. Data management
     1. Information storage and retrieval
     2. Typical business systems
  E. System software
     1. File management routines (e.g., mail systems)
     2. Syntax analysis routines
       a) Command scanners
       b) Evaluation of arithmetic expressions
  F. Games
     1. Simple puzzles (e.g., Tower of Hanoi)
     2. Simple games (e.g., tic-tac-toe)
     3. Searching game tress (optional)
VI. Computer systems
  A. Major hardware components
     1. Primary and secondary storage
     2. Processors
     3. Peripherals
  B. System software
     1. Language processors
     2. Operating systems
     3. Graphic output facilities
  C. System configuration
     1. Microprocessor systems
     2. Time-sharing and batch processing systems
     3. Networks
VII. Social implications
  A. Responsible use of computer systems
  B. Social ramifications of computer applications
     1. Privacy
     2. Values implicit in the construction of systems
     3. Reliability of systems

APPENDIX E
MAYER'S CONCRETE MODELS

MAYER'S (1982) CONCRETE MODEL OF A COMPUTER FOR A BASIC-LIKE LANGUAGE

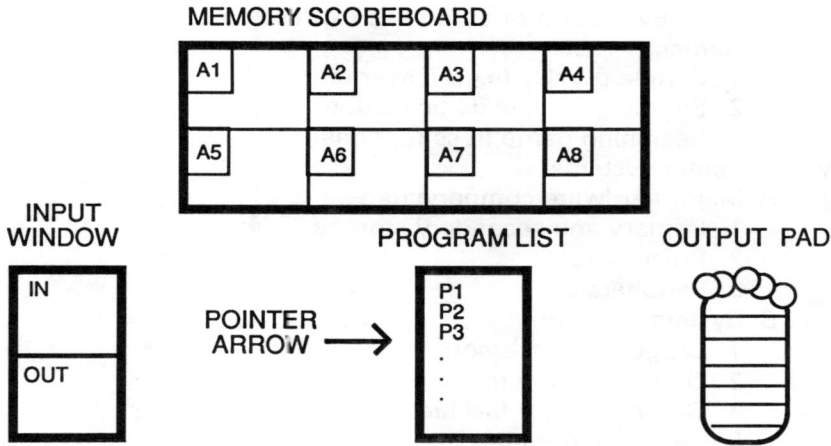

MEMORY SCOREBOARD

INPUT WINDOW

PROGRAM LIST

OUTPUT PAD

POINTER ARROW

Model Description

The figure above represents a simple computer system which you will learn about this in this experiment. The computer is made up of three main pans: (1) INPUT & OUTPUT WINDOWS which allow communication between the computer's memory and the outside world, (2) MEMORY SCOREBOARD which stores information in the computer, and (3) PROGRAM LIST & POINT ARROW which tell the computer what to do and what order to go in. Each of these three parts will now be explained.

Input & Output Window

Notice to the far left is an input window divided into two parts. A pile of computer cards with numbers punched into them can be put in the left part of the window. Thus when the computer needs to find the next card, it takes the top card on the left side of the input window; when it is done with the card, it puts it on the right side.

On the far right is the output window. This is where printed messages (in this case, only numbers can be printed) from the computer's memory to the outside world appear. Each line on the printout is a new message (i.e., a new number) .

Thus the computer can store in memory a number that is on a card entered through the input window or it can print out what it has in memory onto a printout at the output window. The statements which put the input and output windows to work are READ and WRITE statements, and each will be explained later on.

Memory Scoreboard

Inside the computer is a large scoreboard called MEMORY. Notice that it is divided into eight spaces with room for each score (one number) in each space. Also notice that each space is labeled with a name—A1, A2, A3, A4, A5, A6, A7, A8. These labels or names for each space are called 'addresses" and each of the eight addresses always has some number indicated in its space. For example, right now in our figure, A1 shows a score of 81, A2 has the number 17, etc.

It is possible to change the score in any of the eight spaces; for example, the score in box A1 can be changed to 0, and you will learn how to change scores in memory later on when we discuss EQUALS statements and CALCULATION statements.

Program List & Pointer Arrow

Inside the computer to the right of the MEMORY is a place to put a list of things to do called PROGRAM LIST and an arrow which indicates what step in the list the computer should work on.

Notice that each line in the PROGRAM LIST has a number so that the first line is called P1, the second step is P2 and so on. When a program is inserted, the step indicator arrow will point to the first line (P1); when the first step is finished the arrow will go to the next step on the list (P2), and so on down the list. You will learn how to control the order of steps later on when IF statement, GOTO statement and STOP statement are discussed.

MAYER'S CONCRETE MODEL OF A COMPUTER FOR A BASIC-LIKE LANGUAGE

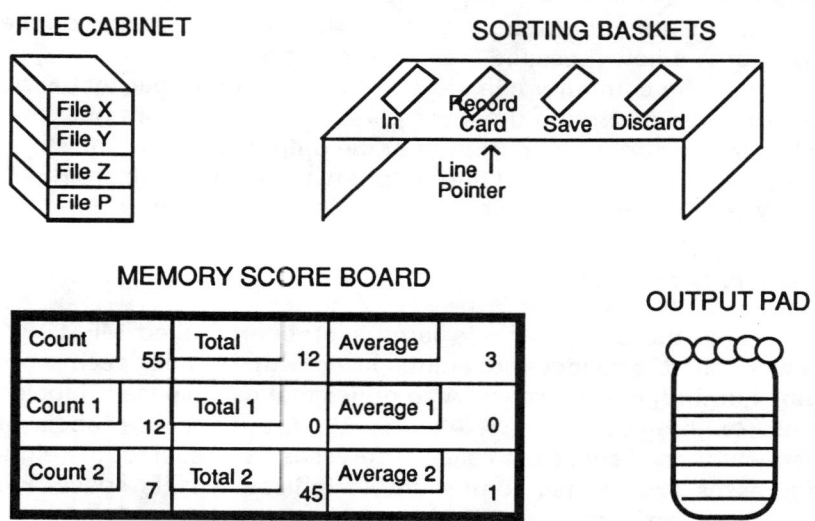

FILE CABINET

File X
File Y
File Z
File P

SORTING BASKETS

In   Record Card   Save   Discard

Line Pointer

MEMORY SCORE BOARD

Count	55	Total	12	Average	3
Count 1	12	Total 1	0	Average 1	0
Count 2	7	Total 2	45	Average 2	1

OUTPUT PAD

Model Description

The computer is capable of three main functions: sorting record cards into sorting baskets, remembering numbers on its memory scoreboard, and outputing information to the world through its message pad.

To understand the sorting function of the computer you will think of an office worker sitting at a desk with three sorting baskets, a line pointer arrow, and a file cabinet with many drawers. Each drawer of the file cabinet contains a different set of records; the name of the file is indicated on each drawer. If the worker needs all the records in a particular file all the worker needs to do is open that drawer and take out all the records. To avoid mix-ups the clerk can take all the records of only one file at a time; if the clerk needs to bring records from a certain file drawer to his desk, first all the records from all other files must be put back in their proper drawers. Thus, a worker may have all the records from only <u>one</u> file on his desk at a time. These could be placed in the "in basket" which is on the left side of the clerk's desk—it thus contains all of the to-be-processed record cards, waiting for the office clerk to look at them.

In the middle of the desk is a work area with a line pointer arrow; the clerk may place only one card in the work area at a time, and the pointer arrow points to just one line at a time. To the right are two more baskets—the "save basket" and the "discard basket." If a record card passes the clerk's inspection, it is placed on top of the pile of cards in the "save basket"; but if it fails, it is placed on top of the pile of cards in the "discard basket."

The procedure the office worker uses is to take the top card from the "in basket", place it in the work area with a pointer arrow aimed at one line, and, based on inspection of this line, to move that card to either the "save" or "discard basket." The worker continues until all of the records in the "in basket" have been processed, so that the "in basket" is empty and the "save" and "discard baskets" contain all the records; then sometimes the worker might be asked to take the pile in either the "save" or the "discard basket" and put them in the "in basket" for further processing.

To understand the memory function of the computer, think of a memory scoreboard. The scoreboard consists of 15 rectanglar spaces, like a classroom blackboard divided into 15 spaces. Each space has a label such as COUNT1, and each space has one number (of any length) in it. The office worker may count all the records that have been stored in the SAVE basket, and this number could be stored in one of the spaces on the scoreboard. When a new number is stored in a space on the scoreboard, the old number is erased. However, when the office worker copies a number from one of the memory spaces onto the output pad the number is not erased.

To understand the output function of the computer, think of a telephone message pad. To communicate with the outside world the computer can write one piece of information on each line of the pad. If it fills all the lines on one page, it just turns to the next page and begins with the top line. The office worker may write down two kinds of information on the output pad: a number may be copied from one of the spaces on the scoreboard onto the pad (but this does not alter the number on the scoreboard), or information that is on each card in the SAVE basket can be copied onto the output pad.

BIBLIOGRAPHY

Augarten, Stan. 1984. *Bit by bit: An illustrated history of computers.* New York: Ticknor and Fields.

Ausubel, David P., Joseph D. Novak, and Helen Hanesian. 1978. *Educational psychology: A cognitive view.* 2nd Edition. New York: Holt, Rinehart and Winston.

Bayman, Pirays and Richard E. Mayer. 1982. *Novice user's misconceptions of BASIC programming statements.* Santa Barbara, California: California University, Report No. 82–1. ED 238 395.

Becker, Henry Jay. 1986a. *Instructional uses of school computers: Reports from the 1985 National Survey,* Baltimore, Maryland: Center for Social Reorganization of Schools, John Hopkins University. no. 1.

Becker, Henry Jay. 1986b. *Instructional uses of school computers: Reports from the 1985 national survey.* The John Hopkins University, no. 2, (August) .

Becker, Henry Jay. 1987. The importance of a methodology that maximizes falsifiability: Its applicability to research about LOGO. *Educational Researcher* 16 (June-July), no. 5.

Better BASIC (computer software). 1984. Norwood, Massachusetts: Summit Software.

Black, John B., Karen Swan and Daniel L. Schwartz. 1988. Developing thinking skills with computers. *Teacher College Record* 89 (Spring), no. 3.

Bohm, Corrado and Guiseppe Jacopini. 1966. Flow diagrams, Turing machines and languages with only two formations. *Communications of the Association for Computing Machinery* 9 (May), no. 5.

Bonar, Jeffrey and Elliot Soloway. 1985. Pre-programming knowledge: A major source of misconceptions in novice programmers. University of Pittsburgh. ED 258 805.

Boudrot, Thomas E. and Jane Switzer. 1986. In search of a computer literacy textbook. *The Computing Teacher* 13 (June), no. 9.

Boyer, Ernest L. 1983. *High school: A report on secondary education in America.* New York: Harper & Row.

Braswell, James S. 1984. Advanced placement computer science, *Mathematics Teacher* 77 (May), no. 5.

Broadwell, Martin M. 1980. *The lecture method of instruction: The instructional design library 27.* Englewood Cliffs, New Jersey: Educational Technology Publications.

Bukoski, William J. anc Arthur L. Korotkin, 1976. Computing activities in secondary education. *Educational Technology.* 16 (January), no. 1.

Campbell, Sally. 1984. *Microcomputer software design: How to develop complex application programs.* Englewood Cliffs, New Jersey: Prentice-Hall Inc.

Carus, M. Blouke. 1986. *Introductory remarks: Symposium on state initiatives for textbook reform.* Paper presented at the Annual Meeting of the American Educational Research Associates. San Francisco, California.

Cazden, Courtney B. 1986. Classroom discourse. In *Handbook of Research on Teaching* (3rd ed.). Edited by Merlin C. Wittrock. New York: Macmillian Publishing Company.

Clark, Richard E. 1985. Confounding in educational computing research, *Journal of Educational Computing Research* 1, no. 2.

Clements, Douglas H. 1986. Effects of LOGO and CAI environments on cognition and creativity. *Journal of Educational Psychology* 78, no. 4.

Clements, Douglas H. and Dominic F. Gullo. 1984. Effects of computer programming on young children's cognition. *Journal of Educational Psychology* 76, no. 6.

Cohen, Rina. 1987. Implementing LOGO in the grade two classroom: Acquisition of basic programming concepts. *Journal of Computer-Based Instruction* 14 (Autumn), no. 4.

Culbertson, Jack A. 1986. Whither computer literacy? in *Microcomputers and Education.* Eighty-fifth Yearbook of the National Society for the Study of Education-Part I. Edited by Jack A. Culbertson and Luvern L. Cunningham. Chicago, Illinois: National Society of Education.

Dalbey, John and Marcia C. Linn. 1985. The demands and requirements of computer programming: A literature review. *Journal of Educational Computing Research* 1, no. 3.

Davis, Ben. 1988. Image learning: Higher education and interactive video disc. *Teacher College Record* 89 (Spring), no. 3.

Desberg, Peter, Diane Henschel and Craig Marshall. 1981. *The effect of humor on retention of lecture material.* Paper presented at the Annual Meeting of the American Psychological Association. Montreal, Canada.

Dijkstra, Edsger W. 1965. Programming considered as a human activity. *Proceedings of the 1965 IFIP Congress* (Amsterdam, The Netherlands: North-Holland Publishing Co., 1965). In *Classics in Software Engineering.* Edited by Edward Nash Yourdon. New York: Yourdon Press.

Dijkstra, Edsger W. 1968. GOTO statement considered harmful. *Communications of the Association of Computing Machinery* 11 (March), no. 3.

duBoulay, Benedict. 1986. Some difficulties of learning to program. *Journal of Educational Computing Research* 2, no. 1.

duBoulay, Benedict and T. O'Shea. 1976. *How to work the LOGO machine.* University of Edinburgh. Department of Artificial Intelligence. Paper no. 4.

Dudley-Marling, Curt and Ronald D. Owston. 1988. Using microcomputers to teach problem solving: A critical review. *Educational Technology* 28 (July), no. 7.

Electronic Learning. 1987. *Educational technology 1987: A report on EL's Seventh Annual Survey of the states.* 7 (October), no. 2.

ExperPro Logo (computer software). Santa Barbara, California: ExperTelligence, Inc.

Farr, Roger and Michael A, Tulley. 1985. Do adoption committees perpetuate mediocre textbooks? *Phi Delta Kappan* 66 (March), no. 7.

Feurzeig, W., S. Papert, M. Bloom, R. Grant, and C. Solomon. 1969. *Programming-languages as a conceptual framework for teaching mathematics.* Cambridge, Massachusetts: Bolt Beranek and Newman, Inc., Report No. 1889. ED 038 034.

Fischer, Michael. 1988. Two pascals for the IIGS. *A+ Magazine* 6 (May), no. 5.

Gagne, Robert M. and E. C. Smith. 1962. A study of the effect of verbalization on problem solving. *Journal of Experimental Psychology* 63 January, no. 1.

Gallup, Alex M. 1984. The 16th annual Gallup Poll of public's attitude towards the public schools. *Phi Delta Kappan* 66 (September), no. 1.

Gallup, Alex M. 1985. The 17th annual Gallup Poll of public's attitude towards the public schools. *Phi Delta Kappan* 67 (September), no. 1.

Garland, Stephen. 1984. BASIC. *Abacus* 1, no. 4, 1984.

Harvey, Brian. 1987. Finding the best LOGO for your students. *Classroom Computer Learning* 7 (April), No. 7.

Harvey, Francis A. 1986. Using template programs to teach structured BASIC programming. In *Proceedings of the National Educational Computing Conference 1986.* San Diego, California.

Hutchins, Edwin. 1986. *Metaphors for interface design.* Paper presented at NATO-sponsored Workshop on Multimodal dialogues including voice, Venaco, France. ED 287 460.

Jahns, Karl. 1985. *Structured BASIC development system.* Unpublished master's degree thesis. Lacey, Washington: Saint Martin's College.

Jahns, Karl. 1985. *Structured BASIC Development System* (computer software). Allyn, Washington: Edu-Comp Consultants.

Johanson, Roger P. 1988. Computers, cognition and curriculum: Retrospect and prospect. *Journal of Educational Computing Research* 4, no. 1.

Joni, Saj-Nicole A. and Elliot Soloway. 1986."But my program runs!" discourse rules for novice programmers. *Journal of Educational Computing Research* 2, no. 1.

Karel the Robot (computer software). 1982. Morristown, New Jersey: Cybertronics International, Inc.

Kearsley, G., B. Hunter, and R. J. Seidel. 1983a. Two decades of computer based instruction projects: What have we learned? (Part 1). *T.H.E. Journal* 10 (January), no. 3.

Kearsley, G., B. Hunter, and R. J. Seidel. 1983b. Two decades of computer based instruction projects: What have we learned? (Part 2). *T.H.E. Journal* 10 (February), no. 4.

Kemeny, John G. and Thomas E. Kurtz. 1985. *Back to BASIC: The history, corruption and future of the language.* Reading, Massachusetts: Addison-Wesley Publishing Company, Inc.

Kemeny, John G. and Thomas E. Kurtz. 1987. *True BASIC* (computer software), Hanover, New Hampshire: True BASIC, Inc.

Khayrallah, Moise A. and Maud Van Den Meiraker. 1987. LOGO programming and the acquisition of cognitive skills. *Journal of Computer-Based Instruction* 14 (Autumn), No. 4.

Kurland, D. Midian and Roy D. Pea. 1985. Children's mental models of recursive LOGO programs. *Journal of Educational Computing Research* 1, no. 2.

Kurland, D. Midian, Roy D. Pea, Catherine Clement, and Ronald Mawby. 1986. A study of the development of programming ability and thinking skills in high school students. *Journal of Educational Computing Research* 2, no. 4.

Linn, Marcia C. 1985. The cognitive consequences of programming instruction in classrooms. *Educational Researcher* 14 (May), no. 5.

LogoWriter (computer software). 1986. New York: Logo Computer Systems Inc.

Luehrmann, Arthur. 1981. Computer literacy—What should it be? *The Mathematics Teacher.* 74 (December), no. 9.

Luehrmann, Arthur. 1982. Don't feel bad about teaching BASIC. *Electronic Learning* 2 (September), no. 1.

Luehrmann, Arthur. 1984a. Structured programming in BASIC, Part 1: Top-down BASIC. *Creative Computing* 10 (May), no. 5.

Luehrmann, Arthur. 1984b. Structured programming in BASIC, Part 2: Control blocks. *Creative Computing* 10 (June), no. 6.

Luehrmann, Arthur. 1984c. Structured programming in BASIC, Part 3: An application. *Creative Computing* 10 (July), no. 7.

Luehrmann, Arthur. 1984d. Structured programming in BASIC, Part 4: ANSI BASIC, Macintosh BASIC, and True BASIC. Creative Computing 10 (September), no. 9.

Luehrmann, Arthur and Herbert Peckham. 1986. *Computer literacy—a hands-on approach.* New York: Mc-Graw Hill Book Company.

Martin, James and Carma McClure. 1983. *Software maintenance:*

The problem and its solutions. Englewood Cliffs, New Jersey: Prentice-Hall, Inc.

Martinez, Michael E. and Nancy A. Mead. 1988. *Computer competence: The first national assessment.* Princeton, New Jersey: Educational Testing Service.

Massachusetts Institute of Technology. 1977. Assessment and documentation of a children's computer laboratory. Cambridge, Massachusetts. ED 207 239.

Masterson, Fred A. 1984. Languages for students. *Byte* 9 (June), no. 6.

Mayer, Richard E. 1979. A psychology of learning BASIC, *Communications of the Association for Computing Machinery* 22 (November), no. 11.

Mayer, Richard E. 1980. Elaboration techniques for technical text: An experimental test of the learning strategy hypothesis. *Journal of Educational Psychology* 72 (December), No. 6.

Mayer, Richard E. 1982. *Diagnosis and remediation of computer programming skill for creative problem solving. Volume 1: Description of research methods and results. Final Report.* Santa Barbara, California: University of California. ED 230199.

Moursund, David. 1983–84. LOGO frightens me. *The Computing Teacher* 11 (December-January), no. 5.

Moursund, David. 1986. LOGO revisited. *The Computing Teacher* 13 (March), no. 6.

Mundie, David A. 1978. In praise of Pascal. *Byte* 3 (August), no. 8.

Nassi, I. and B. Shneiderman. 1973. Flowcharting techniques for structured programming, *Association for Computing Machinery SIGPLAN Notices* 8 (August), No. 8.

National Association of State Directors of Teacher Education and Certification. 1981. *Standards for State Approval of Teacher Education.* Salt Lake City, Utah.

National Council of Teachers of Mathematics. 1980. *An agenda for action: Recommendations for school mathematics for the 1980s.* Reston, Virginia: National Council of Teachers of Mathematics.

Norton, Priscilla. 1988. In search of a computer curriculum. *Educational Technology* 28 (March), no. 3.

Object LOGO (computer software). 1986. Cambridge, Massachusetts: Coral Software Corporation.

Orca Pascal (computer software). Albuquerque, New Mexico: The Byte Works, Inc.

Owen, David. 1987. *Direct manipulation and procedural reasoning.* Paper presented at the International Conference on Human-Computer Interaction. Honolulu, Hawaii. ED 287 454.

Papert, Seymour. 1980. *Mindstorms: children, computers, and powerful ideas.* New York: Basic Books, Inc.

Papert, Seymour. 1987. Computer criticism vs. technocentric thinking. *Educational Researcher* 16 (January-February), no. 1.

Papert, Seymour, Daniel Watt, Andrea diSessa, and Silvia Weir. 1979. *Final report of the Brookline LOGO project, Part 2: Project summary and data analysis.* Cambridge, Massachusetts: Massachusetts Institute of Technology. ED 196 423.

Pea, Roy D. 1986. Language-independent conceptual "bugs" in novice programming. *Journal of Educational Computing Research* 2, no. 1.

Pea, Roy D. 1987. The aims of software criticism: Reply to Professor Papert. *Educational Researcher* 16 (June-July), no. 5.

Pea, Roy D. and D. Midian Kurland. 1984. LOGO programming and the development of planning skills: Report no. 16. New York: Bank Street College. ED 249 930.

Peelle, Howard A. 1983. Computer metaphors: Approaches to computer literacy for educators. Computer Education 7, no. 2.

Poole, Lon with Martin McNiff and Steven Cook. 1981. *Apple II user's guide* Berkeley, California: Osborne/McGraw-Hill.

Putnam, Ralph T., D. Sleeman, Juliet A. Baxter, and Laiani K. Kuspa. 1986. A summary of misconceptions of high school BASIC programmers, *Journal of Educational Computing Research* 2, no. 4.

Quick BASIC (computer software). 1987. Redmond, Washington: Microsoft Corporation.

Ralston, Anthony and Edwin D. Reilly, Jr. eds. 1983. *Encyclopedia of computer science and engineering.* 2nd Edition New York: Van Nostrand Reinhold Co.

Richards, John P. 1982. Homework. In *Encyclopedia of Educational*

Research 5th edition. Edited by Harold E. Mitzel. New York: Macmillian Publishing Co. Inc.

Rubincam, Irvin. 1987. Frequently cited authors in the literature on computer applications to education. *Journal of Computer-Based Instruction* 14 (Autumn), no. 4.

Sales, Gregory C. 1985. Design considerations for planning a computer classroom. *Educational Technology* 25 (May), no. 5.

Salomon, Gavriel and D. N. Perkins. 1987. Transfer of cognitive skills from programming: When and how. *Journal of Educational Computing Research* 3, no. 2.

Sammet, Jean E. 1969. *Programming languages: History and fundamentals.* Englewood Cliffs, NJ: Prentice-Hall.

Seidman, Robert H. 1981. *The effect of learning a computer programming language on the logical reasoning of school children.* Paper presented at the Annual Meeting of the American Educational Research Association, Los Angeles, CA.

Shammas, Namir Clement. 1986. Pascal for the IBM PC. *Byte* 11 (December), no. 13.

Shneiderman, Ben. 1980. Group processes in programming. *Datamation* 26 (January), no. 1.

Shneiderman, Ben, Richard Mayer, Don McKay, and Peter Heller. 1977. Experimental investigations of the utility of detailed flowcharts in programming. *Communications of the Association for Computing Machinery* 20 (June), no. 6.

Sleeman, D., Ralph T. Putnam, Juliet Baxter, and Laiani Kuspa. 1986. Pascal and high school students: A study of errors. *Journal of Educational Computing Research* 2, no. 1.

Solomon, M. 1978. Textbook selection committees: What teachers can do. *Learning* 6, no. 7.

Soloway, E., J. Bonar, J. Barth, E. Rubin, and B. Woolf. 1981. Programming and cognition: Why your students write those crazy programs. *Proceedings of the National Educational Computing Conference.* Eugene, Oregon: International Council of Computer Educators. ED 207 526.

The Story Machine (computer software). 1982. Spinnaker Software Corporation. Cambridge. Massachusetts.

Task Force on Curriculum for Secondary School Computer Science.

1985. Computer science for secondary schools: Course content. *Communications of the Association for Computing Machinery* 28 (March), no. 3.

Task Force on Teacher Certification in Computer Science. 1985. Proposed curriculum for programs leading to teacher certification in computer science. *Communications of Association for Computing Machinery* 28 (March), no. 3.

Taylor, Harriet G. and James L. Poirot. 1984. Computer science teacher certification: Current status and trends. *T.H.E. Journal* 12 (September), no. 2.

Taylor, William D. and Jane B. Johnson. 1986. Resisting technological momentum. In *Microcomputers and Education.* Eighty-fifth Yearbook of the National Society for the Study of Education-Part I. Edited by Jack A. Culbertson and Luvern L. Cunningham. Chicago, Illinois: National Society for the Study of Education.

Thornburg, David D. 1986. A computer language at the crossroads. *A+ Magazine* 4 (March), no. 3

Time-Life Books. 1985. New Languages for Problem Solving. In *Understanding Computers: Software.* Alexandria, Virginia.

Time-Life Books. 1985. A golden age of entrpreneurship. In *Understanding Computers: Computer Basics.* Alexandria, Virginia.

Time-Life Books. 1986. Programming Comes Home. In *Understanding Computers: Computer Languages.* Alexandria, Virginia.

Time-Life Books. 1986. A dynamic decade of development. In *Understanding Computers: Computer Languages.* Alexandria, Virginia.

TML Pascal (computer software). Jacksonville, Fl: TML Systems.

Turbo BASIC (computer software). 1986. Scotts Valley, California: Borland International.

Turbo Pascal(computer software). Scotts Valley, California: Borland International.

Turkle, Sherry. 1984. *The second self: Computers and the human spirit.* New York: Simon and Shuster.

U.S. Bureau of Education. 1918. *Cardinal principles of secondary education.* Washington D.C.: Bulletin No. 35.

Walker, Decker F. 1987. LOGO needs research: A response to Papert's paper. *Educational Researcher* 16 (June-July), no. 5.

Walston, L. E. and C. P. Felix. 1977. A method of program measurement and estimation. *IBM System Journal* 16, no. 1.

Webb, Noreen M. 1985 Cognitive requirements of learning computer programming in group and individual settings. *AEDS Journal* 18 (Spring), No. 3.

Weiland, Richard J. 1983. *The programmer's craft: Program construction, computer architecture, and data management.* Edited by Charles R. Bauer. Reston, Virginia: Reston Publishing, Inc.

Westley, Joan. 1986. How Texas made history with the new literacy texts. *Classroom Computer Learning* 6 (February), no. 5.

Williams, Dennis A. 1985. A status report on computers in schools. *Personal Computing.* 9 (September), no. 9.

Wirth, Niklaus. 1984. Data Structures and Algorithms. *Scientific American* 251 (September), no. 3.

Wittrock, Merlin C. 1974. Learning is a generative process. *Educational Psychologist* 11.

Woodward, M. R. 1987. The use of Nassi-Shneiderman charts and supporting tools in software engineering education. *Computer Education* 11, no. 4.

Yourdon, Nash. 1979. Classics in software engineering. New York: Yourdon Press.

INDEX

ACM (See Association for Computing Machinery)
Advanced organizers, lecturing, 158
Advanced Placement Computer Science, Pascal, 114–15
Allen, Paul, Microsoft BASIC, 106
Allison, Dennis, Tiny Basic, 106
Alphanumeric characters,
  string conversion, 40–41
  string manipulation, 39–40
Analogy,
  caveat on the use of, 165
  desktop, 165–66
  engineering, 165
  mailbox, 28
  mind, 165
  neighborhood, 28–29
  review of, 166
  use in lecture, 163–66
  for user interface, 165–66
Anecdotes, use in lecture, 162–63
ANSI BASIC, 107
Apple GS, Pascal, 116
Apple II,
  early use of computers, 6–7
  Pascal, 116
  storage of variables, 29
Applications software,
  capacity, 50
  compatibility, 49
  friendliness, 48–49
  selection of, 48
Argument passing, subroutines, 46
Arrays, lists and tables, 46–47
Assessment, evaluation, 154
Assignments,
  homework, 150–51
  laboratory, 151–53
Association for Computing Machinery,
  certification 12
  objectives, 141–42
Augarten, Stan, repetition, 34
Ausubel, David P.,
  advanced organizer, 158
  analogies in lecture, 163
  concrete operational thought, 34
  elaboration, 148
  exposition, 148
  learning principle, 148

Babbage, Charles, repetition, 34
Barth, J., parallelism bug, 22

BASIC,
  controversy, 99–100
  early use of computers, 5
  design of language, 21, 105–6
  global variables in, 46
  in the Junior high school, 19
  knowledge of hardware, 21
  National Council of Teachers of Mathematics, 101
  options, 108–9
  preparation teachers, 19
  pros and cons, 103–4
  selection of textbooks, 170
  spaghetti code, 104
  status of, 109
  unconditional branching, 23
  use of, 103
  variations due to variable types, 30
  versus LOGO, 135–37
  versus Pascal, 135–37
Baxter, Juliet A.,
  assigning values to variables, 30, 31–34
  limits of loops, 36–37
Bayman, Pirays, errors of novices with variables, 31–34
Becker, Henry Jay,
  availability of computers, 3
  criticism of LOGO, 130
  instructional computer time, 9–10
  number of computers in schools, 2
  scheduling of laboratory, 174–75
  use of LOGO, 109, 111
Better BASIC, 108
Black, John B., problem solving and LOGO, 121–22
Black box analogy, 161, 164
Bloom, M., early development of LOGO, 133
Bohm, Corrado, control functions, 65
Bonar, Jeffrey,
  parallelism bug, 22
  problems with natural language, 21
Boudrot, Thomas E., selection of computer literacy textbooks, 171
Boyer, Ernest L., technological literacy, 127
Brain analogy, 165
Braswell, James S., advanced placement computer science, 115
Broadwell, Martin M., characteristics of a good lecturer, 157–58

215